Jean Brewster Gail Ellis Denis Girard

The Primary English Teacher's Guide

PENGUIN ENGLISH

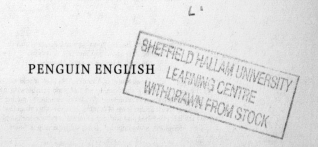

PENGUIN ENGLISH

Published by the Penguin Group
Penguin Books Ltd, 27 Wrights Lane, London W8 5TZ, England
Penguin Books USA Inc., 375 Hudson Street, New York, New York 10014, USA
Penguin Books Australia Ltd, Ringwood, Victoria, Australia
Penguin Books Canada Ltd, 10 Alcorn Avenue, Toronto, Ontario, Canada M4V 3B2
Penguin Books (NZ) Ltd, 182–190 Wairau Road, Auckland 10, New Zealand

Penguin Books Ltd, Registered Offices: Harmondsworth, Middlesex, England

First published in French, 1991
This edition published in 1992
1 3 5 7 9 10 8 6 4 2

Text copyright © Jean Brewster, Gail Ellis and Denis Girard, 1991, 1992
Illustrations copyright © Joan Farmer, 1992
All rights reserved

The moral right of the authors and illustrator has been asserted

Translated by Valerie Grundy
Designed by Jacky Wedgwood
Illustrations by James Val/Joan Farmer Artists and Jacky Wedgwood

Acknowledgements

The publisher would like to thank all those who have granted permission to reproduce extracts
from the following copyright material.
The Big Sleep by Raymond Chandler (pp. 61–2), published by Hamish Hamilton Ltd, 1988 (p. 199).
Chatterbox by Derek Strange and J. A. Holderness, published by Oxford University Press, 1989 (p.
116, 151). *Dick Tracy Casebook*, Copyright © by Tribune Media Services reprinted by permission of
Editors Press Service Inc., published by Penguin Books Ltd, 1990 (p. 200). *Early Bird* by David
Vale, published by Cambridge University Press, 1990 (p. 116). *The Elephant and the Bad Baby*
by Elfrida Vipont and Raymond Briggs, Text copyright © Elfrida Vipont, 1969, Illustrations
copyright © Raymond Briggs, 1969, first published by Hamish Hamilton Children's Books, 1969
(p. 166). *English Today! Pupil's Book 1* by D. H. Howe, published by Oxford University Press, 1985
(pp. 116, 149). *Getting a Young Tongue round the achtung* by Kay Smith, © The Guardian, published
in the Education Guardian, 29 May, 1990 (p. 207). *Jigsaw Teacher's Book* by Brian Abbs and S.
Worrall, published by Longman Group UK (p. 40). *Managing Change in Indonesian high schools* by
Brian Tomlinson, ELTJ, Vol 44/1, 25–37, published by Oxford University Press (p. 211). *Meg and
Mog* by Helen Nicoll and Jan Pieńkowski, Text copyright © Helen Nicoll, 1972, Illustrations
copyright © Jan Pieńkowski, 1972, first published by William Heinemann Ltd, 1972 (p. 99). *My
Cat Likes to Hide in Boxes* by Eve Sutton and Lynley Dodd, published by Spindlewood, 1984 (p.
167). *Outset 1*, first published by Macmillan Publishers Ltd, 1987 (p. 115). 'Run Rabbit – Who
Framed Roger Rabbit' by John Pym, review from *Sight and Sound* 1988, published by British Film
Institute (pp. 196–7). *The Slang Thesaurus* by Jonathon Green, © Jonathon Green 1986, published
by Penguin Books Ltd, 1988 (pp. 199, 200). *Snap!*, first published by Heinemann Publishers
(Oxford) Ltd, 1983 (p. 115). *Stepping Stones* by Julie Ashworth and John Clark, published by
Thomas Nelson and Sons Ltd, 1992 (pp. 116, 148). *Treasure Trail Pupil's Book 1* by Margaret
Iggulden and Julia Allen, published by Penguin Books Ltd, 1992 (p. 152).

Every effort has been made to trace copyright holders in every case. The publishers would be
interested to hear from any not acknowledged here

Typeset by Datix International Limited, Bungay, Suffolk
Printed in England by Clays Ltd, St Ives plc
Set in 9½/11pt Lasercomp Photina

Contents

Part 3 The teacher's role

Part 4 Brushing up your English

Part 1   The basics

1   How children learn languages

Mother tongue acquisition

The ease and rapidity with which young children learn their native language is a constant source of wonder. The experts refer to mother tongue acquisition rather than mother tongue learning in order to underline its character as a natural phenomenon and to distinguish the process from learning, especially classroom learning, which is the result of systematic teaching.

Acquisition begins almost at birth, starting with the first baby noises and cries. By the age of three or four, small children have mastered the essentials of the way in which their language functions and are able to communicate meaningfully with children and adults belonging to their own linguistic community. The innate gift for oral communication characterizes all human beings except for those suffering from a severe congenital disability. This is the case no matter what the language involved, which disproves the notion that some languages are more 'difficult' than others. Neither is acquisition linked to the relative intelligence of individuals, since those who are the least favoured in terms of mental faculties have nevertheless succeeded in acquiring the ability to use their mother tongue. Nature seems to manage to distribute, in generous measure, the equality of opportunity which education systems experience so much trouble in achieving. However, a favourable human environment, as provided by the family, is a condition of natural acquisition of language. The absence of such an environment explains the occasional discovery of 'wild children', who are totally without speech.

There are a number of stages through which children pass in the process of acquiring their mother tongue:

● the prelinguistic stage. From birth to around eight months, infants spontaneously acquire the use of their auditory and phonatory mechanisms, allowing them to hear and produce non-symbolic noises and sounds.

● the production of the first 'word'. This occurs at about eleven months: a sound of the voice which symbolizes something for the infant. It is the start of the phase when infants put names (in their own fashion) to the objects and people around them.

● during the second year, the formerly totally anarchic vocaliza-
  tions of the infant begin to take on the aspect of genuine
  communication as those around enthusiastically ascribe meaning to the 'daddas' and 'mammas' which are initially the
  fortuitous result of the use of the speech organs (tongue, lips,
  vocal cords).

The role of the parents and of all the family becomes more and
more important and exerts an influence which has been analysed
in detail by language acquisition specialists. It is not a question, as
was previously thought, of a simple process of imitation where
small children repeat what they hear purely through the use of
mimicry. In essence, infants create sounds which are given validity
by the reactions of those around them and which gradually
become closer and closer to adult language through the production
of more and more accurate repetitions.

This is how small babies, who literally juggle with the considerable number of sounds from which all the languages of the world
can be acquired, are rapidly led into using only those phonemes
which are present in the mother tongue for inventing their 'words'
and, later on, their 'sentences'.

● Between the ages of eighteen months and two years, there
  comes a point when small children are no longer content with
  simply naming and attracting the attention of those around
  them. At this stage, they enter a genuinely syntactic phase of
  acquisition. Some specialists consider the first 'sentence' to
  occur when two 'words' (groups of sounds which have meaning) are brought together in order to create a new meaning out
  of the union. A French infant who says 'patimama' could,
  according to the circumstances, be expressing an actual 'syntactic' meaning, such as *maman est partie* ('Mummy has gone')
  or *je veux partir avec maman* ('I want to go with Mummy'). The
  succinctness of such infant syntax has been demonstrated by
  American researchers who found an instance where *Dog Pepper*
  could clearly be identified, through the context and the accompanying gestures and intonation, as an attempt to say 'It's
  not the same dog as Pepper' (Brown and Bellugi, 1966).

● In the third and fourth years, the process of natural acquisition
  continues to develop and become richer. This is a period of
  great creativity and remarkable facility for auditory discrimination and for imitation. Whilst the process of acquisition is
  certainly not completed during the third or fourth year, the
  essentials are put in place. The successive grammatical systems

which children construct for themselves begin to resemble closely the norm of the adults who surround them, in as much as these adults have provided the necessary encouragement and discreet guidance, and allowed for the obvious pleasure which children find in discovering language and the world around them.

● The turn of the school comes next, taking over from the parents and continuing and completing the process of acquisition by teaching the mother tongue, in both written and spoken form, and by starting a process of learning which will continue over a lifetime.

Bilingualism and multilingualism

The fact that infants start naturally to acquire their mother tongue from the very earliest of ages suggests that it might be possible to take advantage of this wonderful facility to acquire two or three languages. This would be a considerable advantage in the world of today and the Europe of tomorrow. That this is a real possibility is beyond doubt. There are people in most countries who, one might say, are bilingual by birth. This is often the case of those who have been born into households where two or more languages are in use all the time, as happens, for instance, when the father and mother do not have the same mother tongue.

From the auditory and phonatory, as well as the neurological and biological viewpoint, infants and young children have all that is required for the acquisition of two or three languages at the same time, provided care is taken to ensure that contact with each of the languages concerned is natural.

Sandrine and Stéphane were born in Holland and have a Dutch mother and a French father. From birth onwards, the parents each spoke their own language to the two children and the father shared the 'natural' moments of linguistic contact (nappy changing, bathtime, meals and play) with the mother. In this way, the children simultaneously acquired, without any particular effort being made, both their mother tongue and their 'father' tongue. There was a two-year difference which corresponded to the difference in age between them. 'Bilingualism' rarely means 'equilingualism' in the strict sense of the word, according to the experts and to those bilingual people who have been questioned on this point. Depending on the circumstances, one or other of the two languages is used more frequently and more spontaneously. For Sandrine and Stéphane, Dutch was the dominant language at first, probably due to the greater presence of the mother in the home and as a result of attending a Dutch nursery school. Changing to a French primary school initially reversed the situation but after a time a satisfactory equilibrium developed.

The fears which were once expressed about the damaging effect that bilingualism might have on children's mental development, in terms of late development or even failure to develop at school, have been laid to rest once and for all by a number of very serious and convincing comparative studies. By taking the precaution of ensuring that the contact with the language of each parent is natural, any danger of confusion or of becoming psychologically disturbed is eliminated. The studies referred to even showed bilingual children to be more intelligent (cf. Balkan, 1970).

There is a great temptation to recommend that all children be given a bilingual education given the fact that families who are not adequately informed on the subject often naïvely assume that this is the purpose of language teaching in schools. It is necessary to make it clear that bilingualism and multilingualism are not and cannot be realistic objectives for schools to aim for, considering the limitations on time, the numbers of pupils, and the conflicting claims of other subjects. This is equally true, as will be shown, for language teaching given in primary schools at the time when children have only just left the golden age of natural language acquisition.

Bilingualism and multilingualism are essentially the result of family circumstances similar to those described above, or of other natural forms of contact with different languages, such as extended periods of residence in countries where other languages are spoken, or the coexistence of a national language with a regional language or a language of school instruction.

Countries which are considered to be bilingual or multilingual, such as Belgium, Switzerland, Canada and many others, are not always in a position to be able to offer their citizens the chance to take advantage of this as far as individual language learning is concerned. The languages in question are often competing with each other and reference is even made to language wars. There is at the very least, as Wally Lambert has shown in relation to the learning of English and French in Canada, a negative attitude, not to say rejection, of the other community and the other language which is hardly likely to be conducive to learning.

This was the reason why, in 1965, a group of English-speaking parents in Canada, who wished to see their country become truly bilingual, persuaded the authorities in Quebec to try out a programme, starting in kindergarten, of language 'immersion' in their small town, Saint Lambert, not far from Montreal. The programme was conceived, implemented and evaluated by the psychology department at McGill University in Montreal with particular involvement on the parts of Professor Wally Lambert and Professor Wilder Penfield. Wally Lambert described 'immersion' as a programme of linguistic alternation between home and school. At home, the children speak English, the language of their parents. At school, from the start of the second year of kindergarten, they are plunged into a French language environment, with a French-speaking teacher who teaches the majority of the subjects in French, as well as teaching French itself. The only exceptions are five or six hours a week of English taught as a first language, a physical education class, and, during the last three years of primary school, between two and four hours of arithmetic or art, also taught in English.

The Canadian 'immersion method' was judged to be sufficiently effective, especially after the evaluations carried out by Wally Lambert and his 'St Lambert Project' team, for all the other English-speaking provinces of Canada to launch their own French language immersion programmes, following the model used in the Montreal suburb (Lambert et Tucker, 1972). For the academic year 1982/3, the statistics show a total of 115,000 pupils registered in immersion classes. It should be noted that this figure represents only 3 per cent of the number of pupils in Anglo-Canadian schools. The provinces with the highest percentages were Quebec (12 per cent) and New Brunswick (8 per cent), in other words, the provinces where English-speaking families felt, more than elsewhere, that it was important for their children to speak French well. To this has to be added the fact that, in general, the French-speaking education system in Canada did not use the immersion method for teaching English, as the issue of language is not seen in the same light by French Canadians.

These encouraging results are not a justification for supposing that a miracle method has been discovered, which will resolve all the problems of language learning. Recent reports by the government department with responsibility for the official languages of Canada have contained reservations on the part of the universities and the parents of the pupils. The reports insist particularly on the need to continue carrying out research into the advantages, drawbacks and problems of the immersion method. One of the people in charge, referring to all that had been learnt about the strengths and weaknesses of immersion teaching over two decades, believes that it has probably generated more research in Canada than any other pedagogical innovation.

As far as Europe is concerned, only the bilingual countries are likely to find the Canadian experience relevant. An association promoting the teaching of languages by the immersion method has been created in Belgium, *L'Association pour la promotion de l'enseignement des langues par la méthode immersive* (l'APELMI), but there appear to be only a few schools in Western Europe where the method is being tried out for the teaching of English in particular: one in Liège, one in Holland, and one or two in France, notably in the private sector. Luxemburg is a case apart as there is general trilingualism across the nation. In addition to the national Luxemburgian language spoken at home, German is taught from the first year of primary school and French is taught from the beginning of the third year of primary school. These last two languages are the vehicles of primary and secondary teaching. This early trilingualism is complemented at secondary school by an effective programme of English teaching. The citizens of Luxemburg, where the cost of establishing a university system has been avoided, are thus able to choose between the universities of Germany, Austria, Switzerland, France, Belgium, and even Canada and the United States, for their higher education! Such a situation is to be envied but it is difficult to see how other countries could provide such a level of linguistic luxury for their citizens.

An admittedly less ambitious approach, but one which appears promising, is known as 'bilingual education', and involves some classes being taught one or more subjects in a foreign language in which the pupils are already proficient. This approach is being used in schools in Holland, Germany, France (in the lycées with an international section), the Scandinavian countries, and some other European countries. Bilingual education remains a major theme in the Council of Europe's programme, 'Citizenship and language learning in Europe'.

Learning a foreign language at school

In most countries, at least in Europe, children are confronted with learning a foreign or second language at about the age of eleven, except where an earlier start is made in primary or nursery school, something which will undoubtedly become more and more common.

What is this learning like from the point of view of the eleven- or twelve-year-old child? What is there in common with the process of 'natural' acquisition of the mother tongue or of the two or three languages spoken by those in the immediate circle surrounding the child? These questions need to be considered in order to be in a position to respond to those who believe there is a 'natural' method of teaching (as opposed to acquisition). In fact, the terms are contradictory. The most common teaching situation at the moment is one inside a classroom, where the teacher is face to face with the pupils, in groups of various sizes, for a few hours of lessons each week, and which can only be considered natural in relation to scholastic traditions and to the way institutions are run. Such situations are not, *a priori*, the most suitable for learning a new linguistic code and putting it into practice in exchanges which are related to real communicative needs. Add to this the fact that the children have outgrown the most favourable age for the exercise of their auditory, phonatory and imitative faculties, and the scale of the problem becomes apparent. It is sometimes even said that it is futile to try to teach a foreign language in such circumstances. Actual experience indicates the opposite to be true, provided that every effort is made to ensure that the teaching does in fact help, rather than hinder, acquisition.

One of the most important lessons which can be drawn from the period of mother tongue acquisition is that it is clearly a pleasurable process because it satisfies, in a very short time, a child's basic need to communicate interactively with the surrounding people and environment. This immediately poses a problem when learning a foreign language, as the basic need to communicate is already satisfied through the competence acquired in the mother tongue, and the environment has mostly been discovered and explored through the ability to designate, show, situate, and describe (succinctly) – in short, to manipulate. The need to go over the same ground again, as the price to be paid in order to learn another language, may prove a difficult point for pupils to accept. The primary concern of foreign language teachers is, therefore, the creation of as many ways as possible of giving their pupils an appetite to learn. Even if commercial interests and advertisers are, on occasions, guilty of making use of somewhat misleading claims for language courses, such as 'English (or German, or Latin) without Tears', it is nevertheless true that the learning cannot lead to genuine acquisition if there is no element of pleasure whatsoever.

There is no such thing as a pedagogy of language which is not also a pedagogy of encouragement and a pedagogy of discovery. The effort which the pupils put into participating and being attentive must firstly be rewarded by positive encouragement on the part of the teacher, and then followed up by provision of the necessary help to achieve improvement in those areas where inaccuracies occur, whilst at the same time avoiding making any potentially crippling criticism. The more timid, less outgoing, pupils should not be forced to participate actively, and should only be invited to take part when their abilities have reached the standard required for them to attempt the task.

The fundamental importance of the motivation of the pupils in effective language learning is hardly a recent discovery. It is wise, however, to ensure that the interest which pupils take in the teaching they receive is not solely, or mainly, related to the intrinsic interest of the content of the teaching. Listed below are the main elements of the pupils' interest, the common feature of which is, in fact, action not submission.

● A natural desire to communicate, still present after mother tongue acquisition.

● Pleasure taken in playing with a new code:
  – from a phonological perspective (phonemes, rhythm, intonation);
  – from a lexical, and hence semantic, perspective. It is a source of satisfaction to rediscover the pleasure derived as a small child when using new words to designate; hearing and saying *horse, cat, dog* to label the picture of a horse, cat or dog;
  – from a syntactical perspective.

● Pleasure derived from learning and understanding:
  – the meanings;
  – the way the new language functions (the same as the pleasure a small child derived from finding out how a toy works).

● Pleasure derived from discovering, right from the first lessons, aspects of the other culture contained in the new language (songs, nursery rhymes, riddles, short stories, customs and various aspects of daily life).

Teaching methods are constantly evolving, to the extent that, despite the remarkable progress made in the fields of linguistics, psychology and sociology, which inform language pedagogy (or didactics), very little is known with certainly about the best way to go about teaching.

It is the teacher's responsibility to monitor constantly the behaviour of the pupils in order to discover which ways of proceeding appear most likely to result in learning.

There is no doubt that a healthy scepticism for the more extreme approaches, which have often ended in failure, is potentially the most fruitful way of proceeding. A foreign language cannot be learned simply through imitation and mechanical repetition. Like acquisition, however, learning does include phases of imitation and repetition. Neither can a foreign language be learnt by the sole expedient of learning how it is put together and how it functions, but phases of reflection by the pupils on this or that linguistic point are certainly helpful when placed between more practical phases. Communication using language consists of alternating between listening/comprehending and orally producing/ expressing. Insisting, at all costs, on the pupils speaking (producing) all the time, may be seriously mistaken if insufficient attention has been paid to whether there is proper comprehension or not. Krashen is convinced that this is the case, and has always insisted on the need for a preliminary implantation phase of 'comprehensible input', where pupils do not speak until they have demonstrated a desire to do so and feel ready for it (Krashen, 1982). The major contribution which Krashen has made, and this must be admitted even though not all his views are universally accepted, is that he has shown that the ability to acquire language is, luckily, still present at the age of eight and nine. He has also shown that a properly conceived school programme of language learning will necessarily involve another form of alternation: between phases of semi-natural acquisition (which the communicative approach privileges) and phases of reflective learning to help the process. The latter also helps to compensate, by continual development of the mental faculties, for the diminishing of the auditory and phonatory faculties which occurs on moving from childhood to adolescence and which continues through adult life.

References and further reading

Balkan, L., 1970. *Les effets du bilinguisme français-anglais sur les aptitudes intellectuelles*: AIMAV, Brussels.

Brown, R. and U. Bellugi, 1966. 'Three Processes in the Child's Acquisition of Syntax' in E. H. Lenneberg, *New Directions in the Study of Language*: MIT Press.

Krashen, S., 1982. *Principles and Practice in Second Language Acquisition*: Pergamon Press.

Lambert, W. E. and G. R. Tucker, 1972. *Bilingual Education of Children: The St Lambert Experiment*: Newbury House.

Stern, H. H. (Ed.), 1984. 'L'Enseignement immersif en français', in *Langue et société*: Commissaire aux langues officielles, Ottawa, Canada.

2 Foreign language learning in European primary schools

Many Western European countries have a long tradition of starting the teaching of languages other than the mother tongue at a very early age. This has been especially true for children from more privileged backgrounds. In British preparatory schools, where the pupils are prepared for public school entrance examinations, foreign languages have been taught for many years. From the beginning of compulsory primary education in France (1883), the teaching of languages was official policy in the elementary classes of the lycées (the *petit lycé*) where the great majority of children were middle-class. In Central Europe and Russia, from the seventeenth century onwards, an introduction to French was provided by the private tutors, who were primarily French-speaking.

The period 1950–75

When looking at the second half of the twentieth century, mention should be made of the indisputable influence American experiments have had in European countries. The FLES (*Foreign Language in Elementary Schools*) movement was introduced after the First World War in response to the special needs of a country by nature multilingual. It exerted most influence in the fifties, notably in French, Spanish and German teaching. In 1961, more than one million children were being introduced to a foreign language in 8,000 schools throughout the fifty states.

The trend towards the teaching of foreign languages from primary school onwards was not confined to the United States and Europe. Two UNESCO conferences held in Hamburg in 1962 and 1966 were attended by representatives from India, Israel and Morocco in addition to a European presence on a grand scale with Austria, Denmark, Spain, France, Hungary, Ireland, Italy, Holland, Poland, West Germany, the United Kingdom and the USSR all being represented. The Council of Europe for its part was very active in the field, organizing several conferences and promulgating, in 1969, a resolution which recommended that, wherever possible in the twenty-one member states, at least one major European language should be taught to schoolchildren from the age of ten onwards. The discussion of the more significant schemes which follows will confine itself to describing briefly experiments conducted in Britain and France.

The British pilot scheme 'French from eight'

The British Pilot Scheme was launched, at the beginning of the 1963–4 school year, in thirteen selected regions and contained three unusual features. Firstly, those primary-school teachers required to give French lessons received thorough training both in France and on special courses in the United Kingdom. Secondly, the Language Centre at York University was funded by the Nuffield Foundation to design a specific teaching methodology. Finally, and most importantly, a longitudinal evaluation of the project was carried out on behalf of the Ministry of Education by the National Foundation for Educational Research.

The final report of the NFER, *Primary French in the Balance*, was edited by Clare Burstall and published in 1974. It represented the final outcome of ten years of evaluation work. The results of several cohorts of pupils who were taught French in primary school from the age of eight to the age of eleven were systematically compared with the results of pupils from control groups who only started the study of French at the age of eleven. In the judgement of the authors, there was 'statistically significant' evidence to show that the performance of the former group was better in oral comprehension and expression. This group was also considered to have displayed a more positive attitude to the foreign language and to French culture.

The Local Education Authorities could have chosen to take up the recommendations of the report and correct the faults which had been brought to light: namely, over-much emphasis placed on the spoken language and, above all, a lack of support from the secondary schools where it was found totally impossible to form reasonably homogeneous first-year classes. They preferred, however, to focus their attention on the very last sentence of the 250 page report. Despite giving the impression of a careful verbal balancing act, this sentence was sufficient for the decision-makers to put an end to the trials.

> Now that the results of the evaluation are finally available, however, it is hard to resist the conclusion that the weight of the evidence has combined with the balance of opinion to tip the scales against a possible expansion of the teaching of French in primary schools.

The beginnings of early foreign language learning in France

The first experiment with teaching English in French primary schools began in 1954, at the time of the official twinning of Arles and the American town of York in Pennsylvania. A few years

later, the same system was introduced in Paris with the help of
British teaching assistants. By the mid-sixties, a quarter of all
French *départements* were following the trend. Some 24,000 pupils
in 1,000 classes were learning English (or German, in the case of
dialect-speaking communities in Alsace) during the final two or
three years of primary school.

The spontaneous nature of these experiments was in marked
contrast to what occurred in the United Kingdom. In France, only
one 'pilot scheme' was started in the primary schools. This was
initiated by the schools inspectorate section with responsibility for
English teaching and lasted just three years. It was limited to a
small number of *départements* where it was possible to provide
specific training for some of the teachers and ensure pedagogical
continuity. In the case of German, bilateral agreements between
France and West Germany helped to ensure an exchange of
primary school teachers, especially at nursery school level. This
form of very early teaching was wrongly referred to as 'bilingual
classes'. It included the teaching of English but, despite initially
encouraging results, it quickly foundered on the impossibility of
ensuring continuity in primary schools and, even more of a problem, in the initial classes of secondary school.

The sole outcome of this proliferation of experiments, which
were often poorly controlled (a Ministry of Education report in
1973 showed that the number of staff involved had tripled), was a
decision to allow 'vertical development' of those projects already in
existence and to assign to a schools inspector of English the task of
preparing a report on the overall situation.

The report, *Early Modern Language Learning*, written by Denis
Girard (1974), provided a detailed overview of the projects in
France and took into account information from a variety of contacts established with other European countries. The positive results seen in many classrooms were proof of the benefits of such
teaching. However, for optimum effectiveness, it seemed preferable
to concentrate on the final years of primary school. The report
underlined the need to create, first of all, the conditions necessary
for a genuine 'controlled experiment' before taking any decisions
or making any generalizations. A series of criteria were proposed
for early learning and they are still relevant today: trained teachers
(competence in the foreign language and teaching ability); ad-
equate timetabling (five thirty-minute sessions per week if possible);
a methodology which takes account of the needs of the children;
continuity and liaison with secondary schooling; established
provision of pedagogical support; and integrated control and
evaluation.

The lessons of the past

The lessons to be drawn from the past have been described in a number of reports, including the two discussed above. As far as the advantages and disadvantages of early learning of foreign languages are concerned, it is worth mentioning research carried out in Sweden. A ten-year 'longitudinal' study was undertaken between 1970 and 1980 to evaluate the relative merits of starting to learn English in either the first year of primary school (seven-year olds) or in the third year. Lars Holmstrand in his final report rejects the two 'myths' concerning the harmful effects which the early learning of a foreign language can have on a child's development and the so-called 'optimum age for learning a foreign language theory' (Holmstrand 1982). Against the first, he cites the findings of other researchers in the field. As for the second, his point of view that children's natural ability with respect to certain aspects of language learning is relatively better developed than their talents in other types of learning seems perfectly justified. Holmstrand's report certainly contributed to the policy finally adopted by Sweden for early learning of English. It was decided not to start teaching at the age of seven but to make it universal at the age of nine, a decision which has clearly played a part in making English practically a second national language in Sweden.

Numerous conferences organized during this first wave of foreign language learning in primary schools showed a considerable degree of convergence: the two UNESCO conferences in 1962 and 1966 (Stern, 1969), the Council of Europe conferences at Reading (1967), Weisbaden (1973), and Copenhagen (1976), the seminars organized at Uppsala (1972) and Brescia (1979) by the International Association of Applied Linguistics (AILA) and the International Federation of Modern Language Teachers (FIPLV).

These conferences highlighted the following common points:

- Advantage can be taken of certain aptitudes children have in order to start teaching a foreign language at primary school.

- There is no theoretical optimum age for starting teaching. It can vary according to country and linguistic situation. The age of nine is often settled on after trying other ages.

- Early learning of a non mother-tongue language must be integrated into other teaching in the primary school.

- Whatever else may be achieved, the main concern is to prepare the ground so that the most can be made of the teaching which will be received in secondary school.

- The linguistic and pedagogical skills of the teachers are two of the most important factors.

These 'past lessons' augur well for the new move which has just begun in Europe in favour of teaching foreign languages in primary school.

The revival of teaching languages in European primary schools in the nineties

The Single European Act, which comes into force on the 1st January 1993, provides for freedom of movement of goods and people. This act is proving an unprecedented impetus for the teaching and learning of foreign languages amongst the twelve member states of the European Community, as they prepare to cope effectively with the new international situation. The LINGUA programme, launched on 1st January 1990, aims to make the teaching and learning of foreign languages more effective by means of a considerable increase of exchanges. This applies to students in various disciplines and, of course, to language teachers in education and continuing education. Another way of achieving this aim is to dedicate more time in the school curriculum by, for example, bringing forward the age at which languages are first taught and introducing foreign languages into primary schools.

The revival of enthusiasm for teaching languages in primary school is not limited to the member states of the EEC. Ample proof of this is provided by the new language learning programme of the Council of Europe whose cultural activities now involve twenty-nine countries. Indeed, it is an interesting fact that this (provisional) programme called 'Language learning and European citizenship' lists the primary school amongst the four priority areas for which specific action is planned between 1990 and 1995.

In a survey conducted in 1989, thirteen countries in the Council considered language teaching in primary schools to be a national priority. Belgium, Denmark, Spain, France, Italy, Luxembourg and Portugal were amongst these countries, as was Scotland, which has an independent education system within the UK. The Burstall report, which has already been mentioned, did not have the demobilizing effect in Scotland that it had in England and Wales. It is perhaps not without significance that it was the Scottish education authorities who offered to hold the Council of Europe's first 'new style workshop' for language teachers in the spring of 1991 on the subject of language teaching in primary schools.

In 1993, France will be the host-nation of workshop B* on the same subject, following two years of research by the participating countries. After that, Germany and Austria are to organize a second pair of workshops which will concentrate on the issues involved in starting language teaching before the age of eight. Italy is another country which is well up in this particular field. For a number of years now, various Italian regions have been trying out French and English early learning and the latest primary school programmes make it possible to expand this teaching rapidly.

At the end of its 'Language learning and European citizenship' programme, the Council of Europe is likely to have at its disposal a large amount of information on how best to set about teaching languages in primary schools.

It is highly probable that the number of European countries having primary school curriculums featuring a foreign language will increase before the end of the century. At present, this is the case for six countries: Austria, Finland, Ireland, Luxembourg, Sweden and Switzerland. Other countries, such as Germany, Belgium, France and Italy, where trials are under way, will probably have found the answers to the main questions still being asked, namely:

- the advantages and drawbacks
- the starting age
- the methodology and contents of the teaching programmes
- the respective merits of teaching a foreign language and of developing language awareness
- integration into primary school teaching
- preparation for study at secondary school
- evaluation of the results
- who will do the teaching and with what sort of training?

References and further reading

Burstall, C. et al., 1974. *Primary French in the Balance*: NFER Publishing Company Ltd.

* A prominent feature of the Council of Europe's new modern languages programme is the inclusion of so-called 'new style' international workshops for language teachers. They are organized around a single theme and bring together around fifty participants from numerous member countries for an A workshop which is run by a first volunteer country and takes for its theme one of the priority areas. There follows a two-year period of research and development at the end of which a further workshop, workshop B, is organized on the same theme by a second volunteer country in order to allow the results of the research to be presented. One of the priority areas is the teaching of foreign languages in primary schools.

Girard, D., 1974. *Enseignement précoce des langues vivantes*: National Ministry of Education.

Holmstrand, L. S. E., 1982. *English in the Elementary School*: Uppsala University.

Stern, H. H. (ed.), 1969. *Languages and the Young School Child*: Oxford University Press.

3 The aims of early learning of English

A clear idea of the intended outcomes of any pedagogical or educational policy is vital both for the teachers involved and for the pupils entrusted to their care. This is especially true where such policies are introduced on an experimental basis, as has often been the case with foreign language teaching in primary school (in Scotland, Spain, France, Italy and elsewhere). Whilst participation in such experiments is not compulsory, they are, nevertheless, ultimately expected to provide information on the validity of the teaching undertaken and the possible opportunities for extension or general introduction.

Why teach a foreign language in primary school?

This question is best approached by initially considering the importance which modern societies place on proficiency in one or more foreign languages, as part of the knowledge and skills which can help in the attainment of a satisfactory professional life later on. A knowledge of foreign languages is also seen as contributing to as well-balanced and culturally complete an education as possible, without pretending to encyclopedic knowledge.

As far as secondary schooling is concerned, most countries consider that learning a first foreign language should start straight away at the beginning of the first year when the pupils are generally eleven or twelve years old.

One reason for starting to learn a foreign language two or three years earlier (at eight or nine instead of eleven or twelve) might be simply to increase the total number of years spent learning the language in the belief that such an approach cannot but be of benefit, no matter what the circumstances. This fails to take into account two important considerations.

Firstly, the time factor, i.e. the total length of the period of study, must be assessed in relation to the frequency and regularity of the teaching. Experience has shown that relatively concentrated teaching effort (sufficient hours timetabled each week) is better than a little teaching spread over a long period. All other things being equal, a relatively intensive teaching programme (several hours a week) is likely to be more effective than one hour a week spread out over four or five school years.

The second factor which should be borne in mind is that teaching in primary school is, of necessity, not as structured and

rigid as in secondary school. The way in which the foreign language is taught will take account of the methods and the pace of
primary school teaching. A year of teaching in primary school
cannot be equated with a year in secondary school.

The reason most commonly put forward for starting to teach a
foreign language early is the indisputable fact that young children
have a greater facility for understanding and imitating what they
hear than adolescents, not to mention adults. They are less dis-
tanced from the golden age when they acquired their mother
tongue naturally. It seems a reasonable strategy to try to take
advantage of such favourable circumstances, provided not too
many illusions are entertained as to the possibility of bilingualism
which, as has been already discussed, is entirely reliant upon
exceptional circumstances.

The general aims of early foreign language learning should
appear attractive to children, parents, teachers and administrators
whilst avoiding being over-ambitious and unrealistic. This point is
made in the official text accompanying the 'Controlled trials in
teaching modern languages in elementary school' which began in
France in September 1989. It states, for example, that the objective
is not 'the early training of bilingual children' but, more reasonably, 'to prepare children linguistically, psychologically and culturally for language learning' (BOEN, 1989). Neither is it a question
of duplicating or mimicking the teaching which the children will
receive in secondary school, but rather of preparing them to
benefit from the latter to the maximum, without wasting time.

Of the three objectives ('linguistic', 'psychological' and 'cultural')
which characterize this initial teaching, it is probably most appropriate to start with the second and consider what exactly is meant by
'psychological'. A 'psychological' preparation is one which helps
monolingual children make the fundamental discovery that the
notions they have learnt to master in their mother tongue can be
expressed equally well, albeit differently, using other languages,
where different forms serve the same communicative functions as
in their mother tongue. The linguistic and cultural aspects are
discussed in detail in the third part of this chapter.

English as a foreign language in Europe

English is a foreign language in all European countries apart from
the United Kingdom and Ireland. In parts of Ireland, Wales and
other regions in the United Kingdom, Gaelic is spoken in the home
and English is the 'second language', as it is in the French-speaking
communities of Canada and in the ethnic and linguistic communi-

ties of the United States, where the language spoken in the home has remained Spanish, Italian, German, French, Polish or one of the various Indian dialects. However, in those towns, districts and regions where this is the case, English remains the national language and the language spoken by the vast majority, a language omnipresent in the streets, public places, schools, press, books, radio, and television, as well as in official documents. It is increasingly taking on the role of a second national language in European countries such as Sweden, Denmark and Holland, where the use of the national language is largely confined to within the borders, and where English has been deliberately chosen as the main language of international communication. In these countries, English is part of the public and family environment, especially on television and in the cinema.

What then does learning English as a foreign language mean for the young people of most European countries, be they German, French, Italian or Portuguese?

It is a statistical fact that, for the majority of families, learning a foreign language means, primarily, learning English. It is perhaps regrettable that this dominance pushes all other languages into the background, especially those of the twelve countries of the European Community, which are supposed to be creating ever closer links with their partners, cultural as well as economic. This is nevertheless the situation and is reflected in the choice of foreign language learnt in primary school, to judge from the French pilot projects, where English is taught in 90 per cent of the schools concerned. Only the future will show whether the new LINGUA programme, including as it does a number of features aimed at encouraging greater diversity in the languages taught in the European Community, is capable of initiating and developing a more balanced distribution through the use of specific grants.

The interest, indeed passion, shown by parents for English undoubtedly helps create a favourable climate for learning. It may be supposed that many of them will do all they can to ensure that their children get the most out of the experience, including providing any necessary back-up materials and even sending their children on exchange visits to Britain later on.

It is also a fact that English words and certain grammatical forms are present on however small a scale in countries where English is not part of the cultural environment, to the extent of having second language status. To take one example, the English gerund (verbal noun ending in -*ing*) has proved very pervasive and enjoys considerable international use with such words as *marketing* and *booking* or, in the world of sport, *jumping* or *jogging*. Pedagogically speaking, it is easy to imagine how a teacher responsible for introducing English to a primary school class can make use of naturally occurring examples to aid the comprehension of this very useful English construction for expressing the action of doing (verb plus -*ing*).

A store of useful linguistic material can be found in the names of British and American movie stars, sports, sporting personalities and politicians, as well as in certain other English words, such as *sandwich*, which have been part of most languages for a long time. Care should be taken, however, to restore the true pronunciation (a function of phonemes and stress): *Margaret* with two syllables and *Thatcher* with an initial [ə] and likewise stressed on the first syllable! A further resource which can be exploited with children, even very young children is the popularity of *rock* and, more generally, American popular music. Similarly, an interesting and useful source of written English is readily to be found in the magazines and newspapers sold on news-stands.

English may be a foreign language for many but, wherever one may be, it is rarely far away. The skill is to know how to make the most of it.

Learning to learn English as a foreign language

'Learning to learn' has become a basic concept in every educational activity whether the activity is aimed at children, adolescents, or adults. It is an interesting fact that the Council of Europe has insisted on making it one of the major themes of its new programme 'Language learning and European citizenship'.

An examination of the objectives of early learning of English with regard to 'learning to learn' would appear to be useful, as it is particularly at primary school that fundamental learning skills are put in place.

The aims of early learning of English will be described with reference to the three 'learning to learn' elements shown in the diagram opposite where the core **Communication** is surrounded by an inner ring, DISCOVER ANOTHER CULTURE and an outer ring, ANALYSE THE LANGUAGE.

Learning to communicate in English

LEARNING TO LISTEN (in order to hear and understand properly)
Existing methods and materials for primary school English contain recorded phrases for use in the initial classes. These phrases are short and simple and are usually good examples of the spoken language. However, it is primarily the teacher who, by conducting

Learning to learn English is learning to:

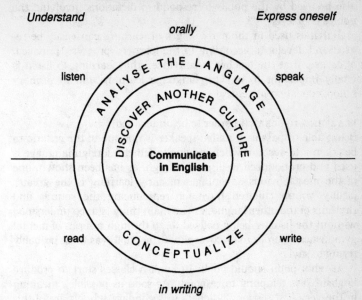

Figure 1   Objectives of early learning of English

the class in English, will provide the opportunity for the pupils continually to improve their listening ability in as natural a manner as possible.

Right from the first *Hello!* (or *Good morning!* or *Good afternoon!*) exchanged with the pupils at the start of the session, it is possible to teach how to listen. Inevitably, the more phonetically accurate the rendering of these exchanges, the better will be the quality of what is heard (pronunciation of the initial 'h', stress on the first syllable, diphthongizing of the final 'o'). Repeating a word once or twice can improve listening ability (and the ability to repeat back accurately); the teacher is not required to give a course in phonetics!

There are other simple ways of training pupils to listen effectively and of checking that the message they hear has been properly received and understood.

The teaching of numbers and letters of the alphabet can be used from the start, as this can easily be developed into recognition games, and activities for checking what has been heard. For example, dictation need not involve any additional knowledge on the part of the pupils (in particular spelling) if it is limited to writing down the numbers they recognize (3, 1, 5, 9, . . .) or letters (C, H, R, A, G. J, . . .).

Visual aids, such as pictures of plants, animals or people, can also be used by the pupils to respond to dictations involving the names of objects.

Activities used in the early stages of learning can easily be re-used and developed according to the learners' progress, provided, of course, that the teacher is convinced that learning to listen is vitally important to modern language learning and to primary school education in general.

LEARNING TO SPEAK (in order to be understood)
Being able to pass as a native-speaker is not one of the criteria to be taken into account when judging whether a foreign language is used and pronounced well, even though, as has been shown, one of the most obvious advantages of early learning is the greater facility young children have for reproducing the sounds and rhythms of the other language. The main thing is to be understood without the listener being obliged to go through a series of mental gymnastics in order to discover what the pupil was most probably trying to say!

At what point should pupils in English classes start to produce English? It is tempting to respond: 'As soon as possible', meaning in the very first session. Teachers in secondary schools are of this opinion. Nevertheless, from a psychological point of view, it is a good idea not to force things and to let each pupil start to contribute when they feel ready. One thing is certain: they will not all be ready at the same time. They will all have differing levels of ability in phonation, imitation, diction, expression and creativity. Some will be more outgoing, some more withdrawn and shy; there are introverted children who are very reluctant to speak. Initially, encouraging the bolder children will help to draw out the more reserved but, clearly, special care is required on the part of the teacher to ensure that everybody has a chance to contribute.

Another problem which immediately presents itself when putting 'learning to speak' into practice is how demanding the teacher should be about the quality of the English produced by the pupils. Opinions on both theory and practice differ and have evolved over recent decades. A very directed form of teaching foreign languages, where everything was immediately corrected and rigorously ex-plained, has progressively given way to 'learner-centred' teaching in which the aim is to encourage pupils to take responsibility for learning by developing their autonomy. This can go as far as avoiding any correction whatsoever of pupils' spoken English, allowing them to express themselves as freely and spontaneously as possible, just as happened from birth onwards when naturally learning their mother tongue.

Many teachers prefer to try to find a middle way between being too easy-going and too demanding. This is a good basis to work on, provided the necessity of being understood is insisted upon. For a message to be transmitted unambiguously and in its entirety, the teacher has to establish the fundamental phonetic oppositions and the correct grammar (morphology and syntax).

She's my brother involves confusion over the pronoun (or the meaning of the noun *brother*) and has to be corrected either by the pupil who made the ungrammatical utterance or by another who has spotted the unconscious joke. If the teacher is unwilling to interrupt the natural flow of the exchanges for too long, the use of the pronouns *he* and *she* and the opposite meanings of *brother* and *sister* can be explained later when an opportunity presents itself.

It would be equally dangerous and counter-productive to allow pupils to continue systematically stressing words on the second-to-last or last syllable. They may be unconsciously adopting the pattern of their mother tongue but most English words are stressed on their first syllable. This is especially important when the spelling of words is nearly the same or the same in the two languages: *orange*, **sand**wich, **elephant**, **cinema**, **photograph** are some examples for French speakers.

Learning to speak in English means agreeing to speak in a way which is different from that of the mother tongue, by means of a game of imitation, supported from time to time by reflection, but with the same desire to be understood.

This fact should be constantly in the minds of pupils and teachers so that primary school English classes really achieve their objective of making learning easier later on, rather than making it more difficult by instilling bad habits which will be difficult to eradicate afterwards.

LEARNING TO READ AND WRITE

Learning to read a foreign language is obviously not a primary aim of early learning of English. Nevertheless, the two skills of reading and writing are learning tools which it would be wrong to ignore, as they occupy a position of fundamental importance in the objectives of primary school education and in the activities of the pupils, who will otherwise have trouble understanding why English appears to exist only in spoken form. It is worth remembering that the failure of previous early foreign language learning pilot projects in England and France was partly attributed to the fact that the teaching methods used concentrated exclusively, or very nearly so, on the spoken language.

Reading and writing (here considered together), not only offer the chance to introduce greater variety into classroom activities, but are also helpful in aiding understanding of how the language functions, as they involve working with the physical manifestations of the language. This makes observation, comparison and reflection easier and is discussed more fully in Chapter 7.

Learning to read English will gradually give young beginners an ability to read autonomously as they acquire both the necessary ability and the taste for reading. There are publishers specializing in English as a foreign language who offer lavishly illustrated readers for children. The derring-do adventures of the animal and human heroes in these books excite the interest of the children and encourage them to read on.

In Chapter 7, detailed guidance is given on how to write short stories which aim to first sharpen a class's listening skills and then to encourage subsequent interest in reading very simple material.

The whole class can learn to write one or two simple sentences which summarize a particularly entertaining episode of a story they have had read to them and partially read themselves. This is an interesting way for them to learn to write and to forge links between the two aspects of the written word.

OTHER ABILITIES TO BE DEVELOPED (in order to learn how to
    communicate)

The preceding paragraphs looked at the four basic 'skills' which are recognized to have an influence on learning and using spoken and written language. They have been discussed in the context of 'learning to ... (listen, speak, read, write)', which are located at the corners of the diagram on page 27.

The development of these four 'skills' constitutes specific objectives in all foreign language learning for the purposes of verbal communication. They also imply other abilities common to various forms of learning, two of which are of particular interest, due to their fundamental role in learning to communicate.

Learning to memorize is the *sine qua non* of any learning process. However, it is not always accorded the importance it merits in language teaching due, no doubt, to the fact that the use of rote learning has often been abused in the past.

The important thing is that the effort required for memorization should never be seen as a tiresome and daunting task, but rather as a sort of game and a challenge, which the pupils decide for themselves to tackle.

Learning a short poem, nursery rhyme, or song, and learning to count are activities which promote such a positive attitude, as is memorizing the names of the characters and the broad outlines of a short story which the pupils have heard, read, or seen on a video. Of even more fundamental importance is the need to memorize the pronunciation (and the spelling, once the pupils start writing) of any new words, as and when they are met within the foreign language, otherwise, new words will not become an enriching part of the existing store of knowledge. The same goes for points of grammar, which have to be first understood and mastered, and then memorized in order that the ability to communicate effectively may improve with time.

The role of the teacher in this continual task of memorization is that of a helpful guide who provides visual and aural aids as well as mnemonic techniques likely to assist learning. Equally, the teacher will encourage various sorts of games, such as Kim's Game, which are fun and at the same time help to develop children's capacity to memorize things.

Learning to create is something of an antidote to learning to memorize. A great deal has been written on the role of creativity in children's general development and on the need for teachers to provide room for the imaginative, creative and inventive parts of their natures. Chapter 1, on language acquisition, has described how children are not limited to just imitating and repeating what they hear, but that they set about 'creating' sounds for themselves, then words which have meaning for them, then phrases, and even a personal syntax which they subsequently modify to conform to the model provided by the adults in their world.

The American linguist Noam Chomsky was probably the first person to insist on the creative aspect of language use and therefore of language teaching (Chomsky, 1965). Imitation and memorization are not sufficient in foreign language learning. Children have to learn to create or invent phrases which allow them to express what they want to say, whilst at the same time, of course, making sure that communication is possible by respecting the rules governing intelligibility.

Early learning of English requires the teacher to trust to the creative powers of children for all the activities of recognition and production, whilst never for a moment abandoning the triple role of guide, ever-watchful counsellor, and model.

Teaching means facilitating discovery, not presenting knowledge. A pedagogy of discovery is one which allows full rein to the enormous potential with which, to varying degrees, children are naturally endowed. Such capacities are a long way from being dulled at the age when English is first taught in primary schools.

Learning to discover another culture

The diagram on page 27 shows the three main areas of 'Learning to learn English' as concentric circles with 'Learning to discover another culture' forming one of these circles at the heart of learning to communicate in English. This helps to underline the fact that communication is the primary objective. It also suggests that the discovery of a different culture (the word 'culture' may seem a little too ambitious) is achieved concurrently with the development, through various activities, of the ability to communicate in English.

Learning to listen, learning to speak, ... are in effect ways of discovering another culture, since an important element of that culture is the foreign language itself. This is illustrated, for example, by the important role intonation and forms of address play in English (*Yes, please* or *No, thank you*; not to mention *Will you be kind enough to ...* which is still very common), constituting a whole set of characteristics defining social relationships, particularly in Great Britain. These are evidence of important cultural characteristics which pupils need to discover, just as they will discover the more informal relationships between Americans who greet each other with a simple *Hi!*, which has, incidentally, become current among British teenagers.

Aspects of the other culture in terms of way of life, people, and places can first be presented in visual form, as illustrations and posters on the walls of the English classroom (or English corner), and can be regularly added to and renewed by teacher and pupils (who may be helped by their parents or their older brothers and sisters). They will also be found in the context of the teaching materials used in class: texts, photos, tape recordings, and videos. All the learning strategies used for communicating, such as observing, reflecting, comparing, and memorizing are equally applicable to discovering the many interesting differences in another culture.

It is best for the pupils to make the discoveries for themselves as far as possible (the pedagogy of discovery has already been discussed). On no account should the teacher give civilization classes! The role of the teacher is to encourage and to help bring about discovery, drawing attention to the fact that the differences in relation to the pupils' own habits and day-to-day lives are to be seen in a positive light as they add to, by definition, the sum of the pupils' knowledge of humanity and of the world. Driving on the left is neither more nor less logical than driving on the right. Special care is required to avoid the development of feelings of superiority ('*Ils sont fous, ces Anglais*'). These are a disturbing sign of a closed attitude of mind and are the antithesis of one of the basic principles of genuine education: to develop understanding and openness towards others.

As the English language itself provides both evidence of another culture and a key to unlocking the differences of that culture, it is not surprising if it is through reading illustrated children's books and authentic written texts, starting in primary school, that the process of discovery of cultural variety can be added to and made more rewarding.

If one of the main advantages of the early learning of a foreign language is that children escape an arid monolingualism, another, equally formative, is that they are drawn away from a mono-cultural perspective and into a broader view of the world.

Learning to think about language
(observing, analysing, comparing, deducing, conceptualizing)

Learning to learn English is essentially learning to communicate in the language and at the same time discovering aspects of the other culture, as has just been described. The reason the diagram on page 27 also contains an outside ring 'Learning to analyse the language' is because it is recognized that a process of reflection of this sort is likely to facilitate the acquisition of the skills and the knowledge needed to communicate.

One possible objection is that children do not have the necessary mental maturity to make and benefit from such a process of reflection. The results of experiments conducted in England by Eric Hawkins, where an awareness and understanding of linguistic facts was encouraged in children (Hawkins, 1984), and of other experiments, inspired by Hawkins and presently under way in other European countries, tend to refute such an assertion, as does the experience of large numbers of language teachers in primary schools.

It goes without saying that this does not mean increasing still further the learning load on children by unnecessarily adding supplementary activities to what they already have to do. Learning to make use, or better use, of their innate abilities of observation and comparison (in other words thinking), is only one more way for the pupils to learn to communicate in a foreign language such as English (along with imitation, repetition, and acquisition of new habits in listening and pronouncing).

Whether it is a question of speaking or writing (in language work involving recognition and reproduction), the children's intel-lectual faculties are being constantly addressed, even if they are not necessarily aware of this fact. Learning to listen, for example, presupposes committed listening and, therefore, active observation of what is heard: pupils must make an effort to discover differences, similarities and relationships with other phonemes, rhythms, and intonations either in the English language or in their mother tongue.

There is no doubt that, for many children, the written language brings out particular points of syntax and morphology even more clearly than does the spoken language. To take a single example, the plural form of nouns may be considered to take the same consonant 's' in English and in French, apart from the variant form 'es' which is obligatory in English after certain endings. This distinctive spelling which, when speaking, requires the use of an additional syllable [ɪz] is likely to be picked up by the pupils if, having first read and written *There is a box on the table*, they are next presented with *There are two boxes on the table*. The simultaneous change from the singular *there is* to the plural *there are* will also provide invaluable instruction for a French-speaker accustomed to the invariable form *il y a*.

Learning to reflect on how the English language functions, in other words, learning to think about language, does not mean taking a course in English grammar. All that is implied is a moment of reflection, if the teacher chooses, whenever the opportunity arises, to draw attention to an interesting linguistic feature. Such a course of action will lead to a better understanding of the way the language functions and result in the memorizing of important rules affecting the ability to communicate.

Seen in this light, learning English in primary school is likely to have a much better chance of being integrated into the general learning objectives at this level and of helping to reinforce learning in other subjects (the mother tongue in particular). At the same time, the children will receive an effective preparation for the teaching programmes they will encounter at secondary school.

The next two chapters set out to illustrate this.

References and further reading

'Experimentation contrôlée d'une langue vivante étrangère à l'école élémentaire', 1989. (BOEN) *Bulletin officiel de l'Education nationale*, nº 11, mars, 1989.

Chomsky, N., 1965. *Aspects of the Theory of Syntax:* The MIT Press, Cambridge, Mass.

Hawkins, E., 1984. *Awareness of Language: An Introduction*: Cambridge University Press.

4   English and the primary curriculum

Children of primary school age are learning to cope with school life, learning to read and write, reinforcing simple concepts, such as number and shape, as well as developing more complex concepts, such as classifying or magnetism. An increasing number of them are also learning English. This presents a special and exciting challenge to teachers in primary schools, many of whom are wondering how they can create the most effective learning environment for the pupils learning English. To provide an answer, it is necessary to discover ways of promoting learning activities which are motivating, interesting, and fun, which at the same time support English language learning.

Many people feel that one of the ways of achieving this is to link language-learning with learning in other subjects. This chapter briefly examines some current ideas about making these links and suggests ways in which the teacher can achieve this.

Why make links between English teaching and the primary curriculum?

Language teachers in primary schools may be of at least two types. The first consists of those who are trained to teach young children and are therefore skilled at determining and meeting their educational needs but are without specialist English-teaching skills. The second type is made up of teachers who are specialists in teaching English but who are less familiar with the educational needs of primary schoolchildren. There is now a general belief that it is important that teachers should have skills in both these areas.

This is a tall order and requires that teachers of young learners know something about educational theory and practice as well as recent developments in language teaching methodology and psychology.

An important discipline in language learning and teaching is that of applied linguistics. Since the seventies, developments in this field have led to an emphasis on communication, including the kind of meaningful interaction between speakers which focuses on the speaker's intention and message. This is a movement away from seeing language learning solely as the learning and practising of new vocabulary and grammatical forms. More recently, linguists such as Nunan (1988) have argued strongly that ELT must include insights gained from educational theory and curriculum development in order to provide for a more 'learner-centred' language learning curriculum. This feeling is an echo of a much earlier argument put forward by Widdowson as early as 1978. He wrote that one of the most effective ways of teaching English was through association with subjects in the school curriculum. In his view, this was the only certain means of teaching language as communication. He also believed that language teaching methodology should link language learning and teaching with learners' everyday experience. His belief was that, by denying learners the opportunity to do this, the teacher increased the difficulty of the language-learning task. This would seem to be especially true of young learners who are coping with so many new ideas, information and concepts.

Also important, both to education and foreign language learning, is the work of psychologists, Piaget and Bruner who believe firmly in 'child-centred' education, where the child's needs and interests are emphasized. They also stress the importance of encouraging children to work independently, often through 'discovery' or 'enquiry-based' learning. This kind of learning is carefully set up by the teacher so that the child is guided to discover facts and information in a variety of ways. It commonly involves the use of problem-solving activities: matching, sequencing and classifying, for example, or making surveys, or carrying out investigations. When using this approach, the teacher has an important role in providing examples and models, audio-visual aids, and other 'support frameworks' from which children learn while carrying out practical activities. The explanations teachers give of key ideas and concepts also provide useful consolidation of this kind of activity-based learning. Bruner draws upon a useful metaphor by referring to these different kinds of support as 'scaffolding'.

In this new field of teaching English to young learners, these disciplines have helped to create a growing awareness of the need to make language learning easier for young children by relating it to their experience in everyday life. This includes school life, where pupils can be supported in their conceptual development through carefully planned activities which allow them to be actively engaged in learning.

The use of topics or themes related to children's everyday experiences or interests is also common.

In some countries, the curriculum guidelines for teaching English in primary schools make specific reference to the desirability of forging links between ELT and other aspects of the primary curriculum. In Norway, for instance, the guide-lines for primary ELT spell this out very clearly:

> When the pupils learn about conditions in other countries it is natural to work across subject boundaries. This can be done by coordinating subjects when studying a particular theme, or by using material and teaching methods from other subjects in the English lessons. (p. 270)

A second example occurs in the suggested programme for the experiment in teaching English to young learners in French primary schools. This refers to the need for children to exchange information about animals, objects, places, and routes (see 1.4 June 1989). It also identifies specific contexts for developing English, such as drawing upon geographical information, by using maps and photos of other countries and plans of towns; information about things to buy from different shops; and information about leisure, including sports, cinema and television (see II op. cit.). This would seem to give a clear indication that the teaching of English cannot be seen in isolation from the rest of the primary curriculum.

To summarize the arguments presented so far, we can see that there are three benefits to be gained from linking ELT to the primary curriculum.

1 This kind of link can be used to reinforce conceptual development, for example, colours, size, shape, time and so on. This continuity gives children confidence and hence is more motivating.

2 The transfer of skills and reinforcement of concepts between different areas of the curriculum helps children to 'learn how to learn'. This includes thinking strategies, such as comparing, classifying, predicting, problem-solving and hypothesizing, as well as study skills, such as making and understanding charts and graphs. It helps to provide continuity between the learning processes established in learning English and the rest of the curriculum.

   (For further details on learning to learn, see Chapter 9.)

3 Language learning linked to the primary curriculum can be used to develop other subjects in the curriculum, such as Mathematics (e.g. telling the time), Science (e.g. how plants grow), Geography (e.g. using maps and plans), or Art and Drama (e.g. singing songs and saying rhymes; creative activities).

What kinds of learning take place in the primary curriculum?

There are many views on what children of primary school age should be learning in schools, as well as on how they should learn. In terms of curriculum content, most people agree on the importance of literacy and numeracy but differ about what else should be included. Many educationalists have argued over the years that the curriculum ought to include subjects such as Science, Environmental Studies, History, Music, Art, and Drama.

The list below attempts to describe some of the key areas of learning and conceptual development linked to various subjects that typically take place in the primary classroom. The list is not intended to be exhaustive and teachers might like to add other items to the list which they feel are important.

Learning in the primary curriculum

1 Developing literacy and numeracy
2 Reinforcing understanding of simple general concepts, such as colour, size and time
3 Learning thinking skills which can be generalized, such as cause and effect, or classifying
4 Developing specific mathematical concepts, such as three-dimensional shapes; length and area; money
5 Learning facts and information leading to concept development in Science and Nature Study, e.g. floating and sinking; how plants grow
6 Learning information about, and developing concepts connected with, social studies (history, geography, the environment, health education), such as families, the school, shops
7 Learning how to learn, for example, learning to predict, hypothesize, or plan; learning simple study skills, such as using dictionaries
8 Developing creativity and aesthetic appreciation through art and craft, and music
9 Developing a sense of morals and morality
10 Developing physical skills, such as co-ordination

Some of these key areas are usually incorporated in published materials for primary ELT or programmes of study issued by departments of education.

There are many different approaches to establishing the kind of curriculum and methodology that is most suited to the learning of young children. One approach holds that learning in the primary classroom is firmly in the hands of the teacher, both in terms of the content chosen and the way the content is learned. This may result in the learning of facts based on strict subject divisions, by the use of workbooks. and by teacher-directed practice carried out with the whole class or individuals.

A second view of the primary curriculum is topic-based, where the content and practice in literacy and numeracy skills is centred around a particular theme which crosses subject boundaries. The topic might be chosen because of the teacher's knowledge of the things the children are most interested in, or it might be chosen by the pupils themselves. This approach can include the use of stories which spark off learning around a particular theme: pair or group work is frequently used, as well as whole-class and individual practice.

Closely linked to this is the approach which includes discovery learning. It is based on the use of investigations carried out by the pupils in small groups, investigations that are relevant to the children's needs and interests. This approach moves the emphasis from the completion of activities which are usually teacher-led to ones that encourage the pupils to work out ideas for themselves. The intention is to promote the development of language and learning processes, such as problem-solving, while also developing the basic skills of literacy and numeracy. In many countries, the primary curriculum is viewed as a combination of these approaches.

Language learning in the primary school is often based on three approaches which seem to reflect the different perceptions on general learning described above. Drawing on the framework provided by Ellis (1984), these approaches could be described in the following way:

1 Medium-oriented. Here the focus is on explicit language practice, including accuracy and fluency, where the practice is an end in itself.

2 Message-oriented. Here emphasis is placed on fluency and accuracy activities based on the content of selected topics; language and content are more closely bound together so that language practice is a means to an end.

3 Activity-oriented. This highlights language and learning processes which draw on other areas of the curriculum; this might include the use of surveys and investigations.

The two most common approaches in primary coursebooks are language-practice activities (usually medium-oriented) and topic-based learning (medium-oriented and often message-oriented). Less common at present is enquiry-based learning (activity-based discovery learning) which uses practical investigations to draw on other curriculum areas and consolidate language already introduced. The latter has enormous potential for reinforcing the concepts and learning processes children commonly need in the primary school, as well as focusing the learners' attention on meaning rather than simply on grammatical accuracy. It is important to remember that the concepts and language used in topics and investigations must be relatively familiar to the children and therefore require previous presentation of vocabulary items and rehearsal of useful grammatical patterns and learning strategies.

How can ELT draw upon the primary curriculum?

We have seen the way in which general curriculum guide-lines for ELT in the primary school may refer to both linguistic and educational goals. These goals are also included in many published materials for young children. One of the first, and still most explicitly stated set of intentions regarding the total education of the child occurs in *Jigsaw* (Abbs and Worrall, 1980). The teacher's guide states:

> *Jigsaw* is an English course for young beginners designed to fit as an integral part into the primary curriculum. It links foreign language learning with the conceptual development of the child ... The English language is used in much the same way as the pupil's native language: to discover facts, ask for information, instruct and follow instructions, express opinions, try out ideas. The subject matter covers many of the topics which may make up the Primary curriculum e.g. nature study ... the calendar ... shopping and money ... (p. 6)

Another relatively early example which draws upon typical activities of the primary classroom can be seen in the teacher's guide for *Sam by Satellite* (Cobb and Webster, 1984):

> "... we seek to involve the children actively, through classroom activities, questioning and reasoning, dramatisation and role-play, songs and games and miming activities." (p. vii)

Stepping Stones (Ashworth and Clark, 1989) also refers to the need to aim for active participation of pupils through physical involvement, making things, and learning through concrete activities. The authors make explicit reference to the teaching of positive learning habits, including organizational and referencing skills.

Coursebooks like these reflect the fact that children of primary school age are reinforcing concepts which they have already learned or are in the process of developing in their mother tongue. They also recognize some of the precepts of good primary practice referred to earlier, such as the importance of activity-based learning.

The most common areas of the curriculum which can be used to develop language learning are:

Maths: numbers, counting and quantity; measuring; telling the time

Science: animals; outer space; how seeds grow

History: understanding chronology/the passing of time; prehistoric animals

Geography and the Environment: shops and shopping; parks; sports and games; using maps and atlases; the weather and climates

Cultural Studies: famous people from other countries; festivals around the world; food and music from other countries

Art and Craft: drawing and printing; making masks, puppets, clocks, etc.; making collages and posters

Music and Drama: songs and rhymes; roleplay and dramatization; miming

The list of guide-lines below summarizes some of the most useful points for teachers to think about when trying to link the primary curriculum to children's learning of a foreign language.

A supportive learning environment for primary ELT

1 Provide a meaningful context and purpose for pupils' language use to ensure genuine interaction wherever possible; this includes providing rehearsal of useful language which the pupils can practise in pairs or small groups.

2 Tailor classroom tasks to the children's points of view by drawing upon their out-of-school experience and interests, for example, by using topics or telling stories.

3 Provide support for pupils by making language-learning tasks accessible through the use of visual aids, such as charts, puppets, and pictures.

4 Involve the learner in action and activity, including problem-

solving and surveys, roleplay, action songs and rhymes, or playing games.

5 Draw upon other areas of the curriculum, such as Maths or Geography, to provide reinforcement for conceptual development and to allow for transfer of skills from one area of the primary curriculum to another.

More information about how to put some of these ideas into practice is given in Chapters 6, 7, 12, 13, and 14.

Linking ELT and the curriculum: topics, stories and investigations

This section describes how topics, stories, and investigations can be used to develop a theme which draws on concepts and other areas of learning in the primary curriculum to promote language learning.

Topics

The topic-based approach encourages pupils to become more involved in their learning and helps them consolidate their language-learning skills in a meaningful context. It is frequently used in published materials as topics provide an interesting way of teaching language. Some of the most common topics you will see include:

family and friends; the body; volcanoes; festivals; toys and games; clothes; the circus; magic; animals, the zoo; our street; weather; films and TV; outer space; food, shops; monsters; famous people.

The popularity of these topics can be explained by referring to some of the characteristics they seem to have in common.

● They draw upon pupils' everyday experience, thus allowing for links to be made between home and school and encouraging pupils to bring general or school knowledge to their language work.

● They are based on the children's interests and therefore are motivating and fun.

● They meet the children's educational needs by reinforcing concepts and learning skills which are useful in other curriculum areas.

● They offer exploration of the factual and the imaginative and the use of a wide range of resources.

You can probably think of other topics which your pupils are interested in. If you want to use a topic which is not covered in published materials, you might like to work out your own language-learning activities. In this case, it is important to achieve a balance between drawing upon concepts and skills with which the children are already familiar and providing work which is not too easy or repetitive. A useful starting point in using a topic is to make a 'topic web' which can help you pin-point the kinds of activities which could be used. You can also work out the language practice and concepts which can be derived from these activities. The general topic web for planning a topic (see Figure 2) might provide you with some ideas on food and shopping.

Stories
Many topics arise out of stories in use in the classroom. The one illustrating ideas for food and shopping, for example, is based on the story *Don't forget the bacon* by Pat Hutchins (1976). For many more ideas on how to link language learning with the curriculum through the use of stories, see Ellis and Brewster (1991).

Investigations
Investigations or surveys provide a useful way of consolidating language learning and can also help to develop concepts linked to mathematics, science or the environment. A list of useful investigations involving practical activities is given below.

- Predicting, counting or ranking
  Children predict the area of their hands and feet; draw around the hand/foot on squared paper; count and rank in order of size.

- Measuring and comparing length and weight; recording results
  Children measure the heights of members of their group and rank order; class draws a graph; investigation of the heaviest man in the world, using *The Guinness Book of Records*.

- Comparing and classifying: recording on a chart
  Children describe and classify animals, using a chart with different headings (e.g. wings, legs, tail, etc.); guessing games based on this.

- Making a survey; recording results on a chart or graph
  Children find out when most birthdays occur; favourite TV programmes etc.; record results on graphs or charts.

- Describing a process, sequencing

Figure 2   A general framework for planning a topic

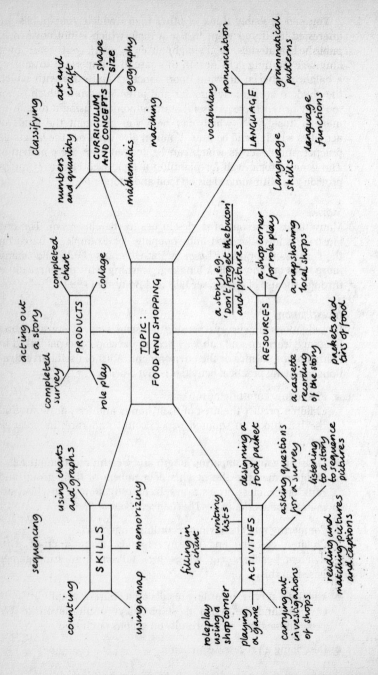

Children describe how to make something; the journey of a parcel; record findings on a flowchart; write an instruction booklet.

- Making and using maps and plans

  Children compare the number and length of journeys each child makes in one day, e.g. to school, to the shops, to friends, etc.; draw these on maps; investigate local parks to make plans showing the kinds of facilities they have for children and evaluate them.

This range of activity types gives scope for children to work at different levels according to their ability and language level. It is important to ensure that the language and concepts which the investigation draws upon are already familiar to the pupils.

This chapter has demonstrated ways of linking language learning with pupils' conceptual development and their learning of subjects in the primary curriculum. This link has the potential of creating a learning environment which caters more clearly for pupils' wider educational needs and interests. The decision to use topics, investigations, or stories to link language learning with the curriculum is inevitably influenced by several factors. These include:

First, the teacher. For example, her views on language learning and teaching; her language level, and confidence in trying innovations; and her knowledge of a range of suitable activity types to develop different approaches.

Second, the learners: their age and interests; their linguistic and conceptual level; their motivation and familiarity with different styles of learning.

Third, and possibly the most important, the learning/teaching context itself: the amount of time available; the type of syllabus and materials in use; and the attitude of parents or headteachers.

Some of the methods suggested here are probably more easily adopted by primary English teachers who spend all day with one class than by those who are visiting English specialists. If you are one of this second group of teachers, the only way you may be able to do this is to work with the class teacher to find out which concepts and topics the pupils have been learning about. This will require a great deal of commitment but can lead to a greatly increased understanding of how children think and learn. The close contact which can be developed through successful collaboration with a class teacher is very satisfying, especially if he or she becomes more interested and involved in your work. However, if you are a class teacher who is interested in linking ELT with the curriculum, then you are probably in the ideal position to do so.

References and further reading

Abbs, B. and A. Worrall, 1980. *Jigsaw*: Mary Glasgow/Longman.

Ashworth, J. and J. Clark, 1989. *Stepping Stones*: Collins.

Brewster, J., 1991. *What is good primary practice?* in *Teaching English to Children*, Brumfit, C. et al.: HarperCollins.

Cobb, D. and D. Webster, 1984. *Sam by Satellite*: Longman.

Ellis, G. and J. Brewster, 1991. *The Story-telling Handbook for Primary Teachers*: Penguin.

Ellis, R., 1984. *Classroom Second Language Development*: Pergamon Press.

Holderness, J., 1991. *Activity-based teaching: approaches to topic-centred work* in Brumfit, C. (op. cit.).

Hutchins, P., 1976. *Don't Forget the Bacon*: Puffin.

Ministry of Education, Norway, 1987. *Curriculum Guidelines*: Ministry of Education.

Ministry of Education, France, 1989. *Enseignements elementaire et secondaire*, Circulaire 89–141: Ministre de L'Education Nationale, Jeunesse et Sports: Ecoles.

Nunan, D., 1988. *Syllabus Design*: Oxford University Press.

Tann, S., 1988. *Developing Topic Work in the Primary School*: Falmer Press.

Widdowson, H., 1978. *Teaching Language as Communication*: Oxford University Press.

Williams, M., 1991. *A framework for teaching English to young learners* in Brumfit, C. (op. cit.).

5 Early learning of English in preparation for secondary school

From primary school to secondary school

In the majority of European countries, early learning of a foreign language is not aimed at achieving the sort of complete mastery which would allow the pupil to move on to a different foreign language or another subject at the end of primary schooling. Only Luxemburg, where a decision was made to conduct its primary and secondary schooling in both French and German, has made the necessary investment in timetabling and teacher training to achieve such an end.

The basic training of the future citizens of most countries takes place over a ten-year period of obligatory schooling, broadly speaking between the ages of six or seven and sixteen or seventeen. Over this period, the knowledge and skills which are judged to be an essential part of such a training, are taught. Subjects such as arithmetic, the mother tongue, singing and physical education are first taught in primary school, whilst others, like Physics and Biology, are not started until secondary school. Whatever the case, the mental faculties (observation, classification, conceptualization, reasoning) and the skills (reading, writing, handling numbers and, last but not least, self-expression) which will influence later learning, are put into place in primary school. Great emphasis is put on 'learning to learn' which, incidentally, starts at the pre-school level in the nursery schools.

There is a general rule governing the introduction of a foreign language into primary school, no matter whether this introduction goes under the name of teaching, initiation or consciousness-raising. Whatever the situation, it should only be considered if the aim is to make learning in secondary school easier.

Despite the general efforts being made to break down the barriers between subjects and encourage an interdisciplinary approach, it is still true that secondary teaching is characterized by a succession of classroom hours (or periods), each dedicated to a different subject and taught by different teachers with their own specific objectives.

This is as much the case for foreign languages as it is for the other parts of the teaching programme, even though the links with other subjects, such as mother tongue, Geography, Singing, Drawing, and art in general, are obvious.

During the three or four periods of foreign language teaching which the pupils have each week, they are asked to set aside for a while their ability to communicate and to understand with the aid of their mother tongue, whilst they learn to:

● understand communications in the other language through the medium of sound (from the teacher, tape recorder or video)

● show that they have understood the main import of the message

● enter into interactive communication as soon as possible with the teacher and the other pupils in the class

● understand situations and actions represented by gesture and image (fixed or moving) or mimed, either by the teacher or their classmates

● express themselves in the foreign language, in however limited a way, taking care to ensure that they are understood, by respecting the phonological, syntactical and semantic rules of the new code

● understand and interpret the way of life of the other country and the cultural differences

● memorize the linguistic and factual content of the lesson each day.

This short list, which is a long way from being exhaustive, is nevertheless a sufficient indication of the difficulties facing the young pupil coming to foreign language learning for the first time at the start of secondary schooling. The task is particularly daunting for monolingual children, who form the vast majority, and whose monolingualism has, if anything, only been reinforced between birth and the age of eleven.

Children who have benefited from a properly thought out programme of foreign language learning at primary school, even if it has only been for two years, are better prepared to respond to the teaching in secondary school as a natural continuation and development of what has gone before.

In order better to appreciate the sort of preparation which is appropriate, three facets of foreign language teaching in secondary schools will be examined in turn, namely: ability to communicate; discovery and understanding of another culture; and the need to reflect on language. These were identified in a recent Council of Europe study (Girard et al., 1988) and were shown to play a decisive role in the language programmes of the majority of countries.

Ability to communicate in a foreign language

Right from the beginning, when modern languages first became part of public sector teaching programmes in European countries, towards the end of the nineteenth century, there appears to have been a universal desire to make a clear distinction between these languages and such dead languages as Latin and Greek. A living or modern language is destined to be spoken before being written (this is the case for mother tongues), thus making interpersonal communication possible.

By turning their backs on the 'read and translate' technique inherited from dead language teaching, modern language teachers have sought, from the beginning of the twentieth century onwards, to develop their pupils' ability to communicate at a very early stage with the introduction of the 'direct method' (where teaching is carried out 'directly' in the foreign language). This was one of the primary aims, although it has since taken several decades and the efforts of innumerable specialists to define precisely what the nature and form of this communication is, and to put into place a system of pedagogy capable of delivering it.

Nowadays, due in large part to the influence of the work of the Council of Europe, so-called 'communicative' approaches, or those based on making communication easier, are to be found in the majority of language teaching programmes and methods in use in secondary schools (Schiels, 1988). The audio-visual based pedagogy of the fifties, centred around the use of dialogue, already had such aims but was bound up in a structuralism and a behaviourism which was too restricting, in that over-much reliance was placed on imitations and exercises involving mechanical repetition.

Language teaching has managed to throw off such shackles and the learner's invention, creativity and linguistic autonomy can be brought much more into play with the sole condition that, in order to ensure comprehensibility, the rules governing the way the language functions are observed.

Above all, the pupils or learners, with their particular characteristics, needs and abilities, have been placed at the centre of the language learning situation, even if it remains true that linguistic analysis is a necessary prerequisite.

Early foreign language learning should provide the pupils with an initiation into learning a new linguistic code as a means of communication.

Discovering another culture

Approaches which concentrate on communication, such as those currently used in European secondary schools, can, if not properly understood, lead to the cultural dimension being neglected. At an elementary level, communication for the sake of communication may result in the cultural aspects which the language conveys being left to one side in order to concentrate on the interaction between speakers and on the manipulation of the code.

Such a view is understandable when it is a question of moving away from traditional modern language teaching where the emphasis is always placed on culture to the detriment of language. This still exists in large numbers of university 'language and literature' courses where the lion's share of each course is taken up by the literature component of the foreign culture.

However, culture, in the sense of the ethnographic and socio-linguistic aspects of the way of life and thought, is now part of most of the language teaching programmes and textbooks in secondary schools. From the first year onwards, pupils are introduced to the real or fictional characters – boys and girls of their own age, their families, their friends – who feature in the sketches, stories and anecdotes contained in the teaching materials (books and aural, graphic and audio-visual support materials). They discover details of life-style, eating habits, pastimes, sports, songs, festivals, and traditions, as well as school life.

A certain amount of geographical detail crops up completely naturally: the names of regions, major towns, capital cities and their famous squares, streets and monuments. Past and present sporting personalities, politicians and film celebrities are discovered in the same way through whatever themes and areas of interest happen to be the subject of study.

The intelligent and enquiring secondary pupil will generally take pleasure in the discoveries which accompany the study of a new language. All subjects, however, contain their quota of discoveries and new material which have to be understood and assimilated. Pupils who are less gifted, from less favourable backgrounds or simply of no more than average ability, often have difficulty in keeping up and tend to concentrate on certain parts of what they are asked to do at the expense of the rest.

Provided it is motivating and not abstract, early foreign language learning in the more relaxed context of primary school has a good chance of encouraging children to take an interest and develop a positive attitude towards the foreign country and its people. This is a result of the impression of participation in a game and in a voyage into the unknown, which young children are bound to have when plunged into a reality clearly different from that of their own world, but where there is enough that is familiar for them to be able to situate themselves. At any rate, this is the observation most frequently made.

Reflecting on language

In foreign language teaching at secondary level, the importance which is placed on reflecting about the way language functions and its linguistic features, differs enormously from country to country, according to whether the dominant methodology favours an essentially pragmatic approach or is of a more cognitive nature. There are extremists on both sides who are under the influence of one or the other of two opposed concepts concerning the importance to be placed on practice and theory in language teaching.

It is a recognized fact that American structuralism deliberately opted for practice by launching the slogan 'Teach the language, not *about* the language!' This resulted in a complete ban on consideration of linguistic aspects and made the word 'grammar' taboo. Grammar was no longer taught, but there was a great deal of practice using the structures of the language which was considered sufficient guarantee of the best type of teaching for everyone.

With the arrival of Noam Chomsky's transformational grammar and the pedagogical applications which some have sought to base upon it, the pendulum has swung markedly in the direction of theory, putting into question the sort of teaching based on the acquisition of new linguistic habits.

The communicative approach has often been seen as a return to practice with a vengeance and an encouragement to neglect once again analysis and reflection on the language.

As is the case in many other areas, the correct path is probably to be found somewhere between the two, by striking a reasonable balance based on the actual needs of different pupils and on their different ways of learning.

Learning to reflect and to understand are, after all, very important parts of any educational activity, and secondary pupils are encouraged to move in this direction in all their subjects. It is difficult to see why foreign languages should be considered to be different in this respect.

In order to teach secondary level pupils to communicate effectively in a foreign language, there is now general agreement in all European countries that it is a good idea to make them aware of the particular ways in which the language functions in order for meaning to be produced.

Primary school teaching of a foreign language should also, therefore, prepare pupils for this reflection on language. This will, of course, be done in as concrete a way as possible, without dedicating over-much time to it, since the room in the timetable for foreign language teaching is generally limited. A few minutes at the end of the session is usually sufficient. The pupils can be asked to consider any particular linguistic point which they may have noticed whilst working on other activities. In most cases, and certainly when first learning a language, the pupils will, of necessity, carry out such reflection in their mother tongue. If there has been discussion on the likes and dislikes of a particular character or of one of the pupils, the third person singular of the verb *like* with its final [s] will have been heard a great deal. By comparing *John likes music* with *John and Susan like music*, and observing the presence or absence of the sibilant at the end of the verb (or of the letter 's' in the written form), the pupils can take the initial steps towards the discovery of an important rule for conjugating verbs. The discovery will be completed as they quickly come to realize that, for all verbs in English with the exception of the modals, the third person singular always behaves in this way. A comparison with the mother tongue on this point will reveal a difference or a striking similarity which is bound to help the pupils to memorize the phenomenon. Similarly, the existence or otherwise of a plural inflection for nouns and adjectives, and the word order in a sentence, depending on whether it is affirmative or interrogative, can be noted and commented on briefly, as and when appropriate.

This activity of reflection on the part of the pupils is not aimed at learning grammatical terminology but at helping them discover, little by little, the rules governing the way the new language functions, rules which they will express in their own words. The most important thing is that they show they have understood particular phenomena, which they have discovered for themselves.

It is a question, therefore, of a pedagogy of discovery which initiates linguistic awareness, be it to do with grammar, phonology or semantics. This has the advantage both of making foreign language learning easier and of consolidating knowledge of the mother tongue.

Quality rather than quantity of learning

The most serious miscalculation which can be made when organizing foreign language teaching in primary schools is to seek to make significant savings in time and to imagine, for example, that by starting the teaching two years before entry into secondary school, the pupils will have learnt the contents of the first year teaching programme at secondary school, taking into account the fact that not so many periods are available in the primary school timetable. This can lead to a temptation to base the two years of teaching on a textbook or programme used in the first year at secondary school. Such a course of action is doubly dangerous because it fails to take into account not only the fact that the learning strategies and interests of children under eleven are different from those of older children in the first years of secondary school, but also the fact that the rate of progress is different. Foreign language learning in primary school should always be seen as a satisfying experience in a relaxed atmosphere and not as a race against the clock.

All this is not to say that no effort is required. Learning (as opposed to the natural process of acquisition) requires an effort and a desire to learn. The teacher, however, should do everything possible to ensure that this effort is freely made, once the desire to learn, to understand and to retain has been awakened. Clearly, this is not just true for primary schools but it is there that particular attention needs to be paid to the point.

To say that early learning must, above all, prepare pupils for the language teaching they will receive in secondary schools implies that secondary school teaching will take as a point of departure a verifiable and measurable level of learning, concerned not so much with quantity as with quality.

It is perfectly natural that the language teachers who take the first-year classes in secondary school should wish to reassure themselves as to the effectiveness of any prior learning, in terms of both knowledge and skills, of the children who have spent two or three years learning English or German in primary school.

This certainly will not be done in a systematic or exhaustive manner. How could it be when, in all likelihood, the primary school teachers, rather than being locked into a restrictive programme, will instead have followed guide-lines placing the emphasis on their personal initiative? Secondary teachers will conduct surveys and, above all, observe the linguistic and language behaviour of the pupils throughout the initial sessions in order to be able subsequently to adapt their own teaching to what has already been learnt.

The most readily observable learning is lexical knowledge which can be checked orally or through written tests, using visual prompts (names of common objects, animals, trees, numbers, adjectives, adverbs of place, etc.). The names of countries, regions, towns, meals, festivals and well-known people can also be used to assess the degree of initial cultural awareness.

Language skills will be most readily apparent in the degree of competence shown when communicating through the medium of the written word (reading and writing). It is recognized that this requires skills as diverse as:

- knowing how to listen
- being able to distinguish between the distinctive sounds (phonemes) of the foreign language
- being able to recognize the patterns of rhythm and intonation in a sentence
- being able to understand progressively the meaning of words and sentences
- being able to produce intelligible oral messages
- knowing how to put knowledge of the spoken word into writing in an equally intelligible form.

Secondary school teachers will, of necessity, be concerned with the quality of the skills which their pupils have acquired in primary school, including auditory skills, comprehension, accuracy of pronunciation, and authenticity of oral and written communications. They will not, for all that, be expecting the pupils to have completely mastered such skills, but will demand that the pupils conform, within reasonable limits, to the standards set by native users of the foreign language.

Early learning is only justified if what is learnt serves as a springboard, however modest, for the teaching to come. Nothing could be more counter-productive than inaccurate knowledge or language skills which result in the teacher making constant corrections and having to go over what has supposedly already been learnt. This is very discouraging for the pupils and can lead to feelings of failure and a negative attitude in place of the greater motivation which was, with reason, expected of an early introduction to the language.

Whether teachers in primary school work full-time with the same class, teaching all the subjects including a foreign language, or whether they have responsibility for teaching English in several classes or, indeed, whether they are secondary school English teachers working part-time as English teachers in one or more primary schools, they should never lose sight of the two facets of English teaching in primary school:

- that the methodology be integrated, in its cultural and educational objectives, into the overall primary school programme
- that the pupils receive a preparation for the teaching they will receive in secondary school.

In order for teachers, especially those who teach exclusively in primary schools, to respond to the second of these objectives, they will find it necessary to take every opportunity to make contact with the secondary school English teachers who will be responsible for teaching their pupils when they first go to secondary school.

Opportunities may present themselves on courses, at conferences, and at meetings organized by school management or professional associations. In conjunction with the colleague who will teach the pupils in the first year of secondary school, it is important to try to set up class visits, followed by interviews.

There is no question, of course, of modelling primary school teaching on what is done in secondary schools. Indeed, the main aim of this book is to draw attention to all that is specific about primary school language teaching.

However, a basic concern with the coherence of the education children and adolescents receive means that bridges have to be built between the different stages of this education.

The purpose of this, the last chapter in the part of the present work dealing with the 'foundations' of early learning of English, is precisely to help teachers bridge these gaps.

References and further reading

Girard, D. et al., 1988. *Choix et distribution des contenus dans les programmes de langues*: Conseil de l'Europe, Strasbourg.

Shiels, J., 1988. *Communication in the Modern Languages Classroom*: Conseil de l'Europe, Strasbourg.

Part 2   Teaching language learning skills

6   The spoken word

Learning to listen in English

The initial stages

Listening to a foreign language is hard work, especially for young children. In the early stages of learning English, the pupils may spend much of their time listening to the teacher while playing simple games, singing songs, saying rhymes or listening to simple stories. The teacher will have to decide how much of the general 'classroom language', such as instructions, questions or praise will be in the pupils' mother tongue and how much in English. It is likely, of course, that the proportion of English for these purposes will increase as time goes on.

An important point for teachers to bear in mind is that children concentrate and listen with understanding more effectively if they are motivated and engaged in purposeful activity while listening. It is important, therefore, to remember that listening is not a passive activity. Always asking children to simply 'listen and remember' places a great strain on their memory and tends not to develop listening skills. The teacher will be able to support children's listening with understanding more effectively if she directs her pupils' attention to specific points that have to be listened for. She can do this by using activities which actively support learners' understanding and guide their attention to specific parts of the spoken text. This might include the use of visual materials, for example, pictures to match or sequence, or perhaps written support or frameworks, such as the completion of charts.

The following guide-lines may be useful when planning how to develop pupils' listening skills.

GIVE THE CHILDREN CONFIDENCE
The children should be told that they cannot always be expected to understand every word. The teacher needs to be clear in her own mind if the children are being asked to understand the general content of a spoken text; this is known as understanding the 'gist' of the message. If this is not the case, she might ask the children to focus more on specific details, such as when following the exact

sequence of events in a story. The use of support materials will help children feel confident about what it is important to concentrate on.

HELP THE CHILDREN TO DEVELOP STRATEGIES FOR LISTENING

An important strategy which the teacher should encourage in her learners is the use of 'intelligent guesswork'. This can be developed by explaining that they can use their background knowledge to work out the meaning of new words, or draw upon any information given in pictures or in charts. They may even be encouraged to notice her body language or the way she uses her voice to stress important words which might give them some clues about the meaning. Some of the most important listening strategies include:

- predicting. It is useful to encourage children to predict what they think might come next in a spoken message. This means that they then listen to check whether their expectation matches the reality of what they hear. This helps to give children success in the task which, in turn, makes them feel more confident.

- inferring opinion or attitude. An awareness of stress, intonation and body language, such as facial expressions or gestures, will help the children work out meaning, especially in dialogues or story-telling.

- working out the meaning from context. Although the teacher might like to gloss new words before the children listen to something, she also needs to encourage them to use pictures and their general knowledge about a topic to work out the meaning of unfamiliar words.

- recognizing discourse patterns and markers. Words such as *first*, *then*, *finally*, or *but*, *and*, *so* give important signals about what is coming next in a spoken text. This is especially important when listening to a sequence of events, such as in a story or a set of instructions.

EXPLAIN WHY THE CHILDREN HAVE TO LISTEN

Make sure the children are clear about why they are listening. This means spelling out which part of the message they need to focus on and what they are going to do before listening, while they listen, or after listening. For example, if they are required to draw something as they are listening. In this case, the children need to know that the words to focus on will be key nouns, along with adjectives which describe colour, size or shape, and prepositions

Table 1 While-listening activities

Activity type	Purpose	Materials
1 Listen and repeat Examples of this are found in games such as Chinese Whispers where one child whispers a message to another child, who then passes on the message to another child and so on. The last child repeats what they have heard and the class compare this message with the original. Some very interesting variations often occur! Other listen and repeat games ask the learners to repeat something only if it is true.	● Listening for details to improve memory and concentration ● Listening with enjoyment to improve listening attitude	Short spoken messages such as instructions, or statements containing no more than ten words
2 Listen and discriminate In this kind of activity the learners' attention is often focused on pronunciation features such as listening for words which rhyme, or selecting phrases which have the same rhythmic pattern. This is especially useful when using songs and rhymes or when using stories which have rhyming sequences.	● Listening for detail to discriminate between sounds and rhythmic patterns ● Providing ear-training to improve pronunciation	Songs and rhymes Rhyming stories

Activity type	Purpose	Materials
3 Listen and perform actions/follow instructions This kind of activity is used with action songs, rhymes, or games such as Blind Man's Buff or What's the Time Mr. Wolf? Following instructions can also be used as a listening activity when the learner is asked to trace a route on a plan or map. It should not be used, however, if the children have not practised doing this in their mother tongue.	• Listening for enjoyment and to improve memory and concentration span • Listening to the use of prepositional phrases, e.g. *on the left/right*; or discourse markers, e.g. *first, then, next*; and action verbs, e.g. *put, fold, turn*	Action songs and rhymes Plans or maps Instructions for games, e.g. origami (paper-folding)
4 Listen and draw/colour Picture dictation is often used to help children focus on key nouns and on adjectives used to describe their colour, size, shape, and so on. The whole picture can be drawn, or a picture which has missing items can be added to as children listen.	• Listening to consolidate understanding of concepts and new vocabulary, e.g. round, square, large, small, blue yellow	Short spoken descriptions which can be accompanied by incomplete drawings which pupils finish or colour in
5 Listen and predict This kind of activity has already been referred to and is particularly useful in drawing on pupils' previous learning.	• Listening to increase motivation and concentration	Question and answer sessions based on, e.g. general knowledge, pictures or the cover of a book or story
6 Listen and guess This kind of listening is often based on the description of something whose identity the children have to guess.	• Listening for detail to pick out key vocabulary used to describe, e.g. parts of an animal's body	Short spoken descriptions which can be accompanied by a selection of items for pupils to eliminate

Activity type	Purpose	Materials
7 Listen and label This activity is used with drawings, maps or diagrams where the learners are asked to listen to a description of an animal, person, or place in order to label key parts.	● Listening to develop reading and writing skills or to develop concepts	Written labels provided for pupils or written words on the blackboard for pupils to copy
8 Listen and match This usually involves matching pictures to spoken words and is common in games such as Bingo. Older children can be involved in activities which ask them to match pictures or written statements to other written texts, such as speech bubbles taken from dialogues or stories.	● Listening to consolidate new vocabulary and structures	Bingo cards Worksheets on which children draw a line to connect a picture with the correct words or written labels or speech bubbles to match with pictures
9 Listen and sequence As described earlier, this activity is usually based on pictures or written phrases which are rearranged into the correct order while listening to a story or set of instructions.	● Listening to improve memory and concentration span Listening to consolidate new vocabulary or structures	Pictures or written statements Worksheets with boxes in which children number the order of details listened to

Activity type	Purpose	Materials
10 Listen and classify This activity is also usually based on pictures. The children listen carefully to descriptions, for example, different animals, which they then have to sort into different sets. These might include sets of wild animals or pets; animals with four legs, two legs and no legs; animals which can swim, fly or move on the ground.	• Listening to improve concentration span and to consolidate new vocabulary and structures	Pictures Worksheets using written words on the blackboard which pupils copy into the appropriate column of a chart while listening
11 Listen and transfer information This involves an exchange of information in pairs or groups. The pupils might be asked to carry out a survey or questionnaire where they ask each other questions and listen carefully for the answer. The responses are recorded on a chart to help the children remember details and to consolidate their understanding. Common surveys are based on finding out about favourite sports, likes and dislikes concerning food, birthdays and so on.	• Listening to improve interactional skills	Worksheets to carry out surveys and questionnaires with columns for pupils to complete. For example:

Favourite sports

Do you like	you	your partner
tennis	✓	✓
football	✓	✗
swimming	✗	✓
roller skating	✓	✓

which describe their position in relation to each other.

Different kinds of listening purpose are described below.

- To improve the general listening attitude: this includes listening for enjoyment, to improve concentration span, or to develop the memory. Various listening games are useful here, such as Simon Says.

- To develop aspects of language: this includes listening to improve the pronunciation of sounds, stress and rhythm and intonation in English, as well as becoming familiar with new words and structural patterns. Listening to learn songs and rhymes provides important pronunciation practice, while listening to stories may provide practice in the simple past tense or vocabulary connected with the topic of 'weather', for example.

- To reinforce conceptual development: some spoken texts, such as stories, can act as useful revision for reinforcing concepts such as colours, size, or cause and effect, which will have been covered in other areas of the school curriculum.

- To interact with others: listening is an important part of communicating with others. Activities which encourage children to work with others, for example, when carrying out surveys in pairs or playing games in groups, require the learners to negotiate meaning by listening and asking questions, checking meaning, agreeing and so on.

- To provide support for literacy: older children can be encouraged to make connections between spoken and written English by picking out written words or statements which are part of a spoken message.

SET A SPECIFIC LISTENING TASK

In order to make listening an active process, teachers need to develop a repertoire of different activity types which 'fit' different types of language. When listening to a series of actions in a narrative, for example, a listening task which asks the children to rearrange a series of pictures, or put numbers by pictures describing different actions, supports the child's understanding very well. If learners are asked to listen to a long stretch of English without visual support and are asked to simply recall the facts, they are in reality being 'tested' rather than 'taught'. Specific activities, such as games used to develop the pupils' memory, fall into a different category, of course. In all other cases it is important, therefore, to teach listening by making explicit to children the relevant strategies outlined earlier, as well as by drawing upon a range of tasks which the learners complete while they are listening. The while-listening activities shown in the chart (see Table 1) give you an idea of the different possibilities. The activities are graded according to level of difficulty although this depends on the text you use. You will probably be able to add activities of your own.

ORGANIZING LISTENING

The development of listening skills does not have to rely on the availability of a cassette or pre-recorded material. Much can be done by the teacher simply speaking while all the children follow what she says with a given purpose in mind and a specific task to complete. Many of the activities described in Table 1 rely on the teacher's use of spoken instructions, descriptions, songs, rhymes, games and stories used with the whole class.

If you do have a cassette of published listening materials, this is useful to provide a good model of spoken English and allows learners, both those who work slowly and those who complete activities quickly, to work independently at their own pace. The materials used may take the form of published materials or may be teacher-made recordings of simple stories with accompanying activities and so on. In this case, it is useful to consider setting up a 'listening corner' in one part of the classroom. It can be created by screening off a corner, with a cupboard or screens, to provide a quiet area for children to listen in pairs or groups. The children will of course need to be trained in how to use a cassette player on their own. It is also necessary to make sure the materials the children will use are easily available and are clearly labelled or colour-coded to show their level of difficulty. The activities can be made 'self-correcting', so that the children can find out quickly whether a listen and sequence activity, for example, has been completed correctly.

Learning to speak in English

Expectations

Most children equate learning a foreign language with learning to speak it and, because learning to speak their mother tongue was a seemingly easy task, they expect it to be the same with the foreign language. They want immediate results and, even after their first lesson, will want to show other children in the school or members of their family that they can speak some English. Young beginners in France were asked what they hoped to be able to do in English by the end of the year. What they said reflected this attitude and also revealed that they expected to learn quickly in order to communicate with other people. This is what they said:

'I hope to speak it.'
'I want to speak well.'
'I want to understand well and reply without hesitating.'
'I want to have conversations with English people.'

The comments show a strong motivation to learn. If children are to maintain this initial motivation, they need to be given opportunities to speak English as soon and as much as possible, so as to be made to feel that they are making progress and fulfilling their expectations, thus avoiding disappointment.

The initial stages

It is important that children leave their first few lessons with some English to 'take away'. It is therefore useful to begin an English programme by teaching children vocabulary for basic concepts, such as numbers, colours, and so on, which can provide the basis for subsequent activities. First lessons often focus on teaching simple greetings and introductions, for example, *Hello! What's your name?/My name's .../This is ...* Pupils could be given English names, although they should be allowed to keep their own name if they wish. Where possible, give the closest English equivalent, or anglicize a name, for example, *Mehdi/Meddy*: the learning of English names provides pronunciation practice. Chapter 11 suggests some useful tips for learning your pupils' names. Teaching pupils a few rhymes and songs at the beginning of their course will also give them the impression that they are learning to speak English quickly.

Chapter 11 discusses the importance of finding out about pupils' previous language learning experience and attitudes to English. Thus many language programmes begin with a lesson to help pupils understand why they are learning English. For example, they may be asked to think of famous people who speak English; where English is spoken in the world; and so on. They may also be asked to think of any English words they know, such as *hamburger, steak, sandwich, tennis, football, jeans, hotel, taxi, television,* etc. Their attention can be focused on how these words are pronounced in comparison with their own language. This will provide a useful introduction to the features of English pronunciation. The aim of this type of reflection is to heighten children's awareness of the use of language and to build up their confidence by making them realize how much English they know already.

Formulaic language

In the early stages of learning, not much spontaneous speech can be expected from pupils. Much of the English they will learn to produce in the initial stages will be what is known as formulaic language. This consists of routines or patterns which children memorize and which enable them to communicate with a minimum of linguistic competence. As this type of language is repeated regularly, children learn it quickly and have the impression that they can speak a lot. Such language consists of:

● simple greetings: *Hello! How are you? / I'm fine, thank you. And you?*

● social English: *Did you have a nice weekend? / Have a nice weekend!*

● routines: *What's the date? What's the weather like today?*

● classroom language: *Listen. Repeat. Sit down. Work in pairs. Good. It's your turn. Be quiet!*

● asking permission: Pupils can be encouraged to do this if you prepare five or six cards with common requests written on them, for example, *Can I/May I go to the toilet? Can I clean the board? Can I wash my hands? Can I put the book away?* etc. Attach these to a board at the front of the class. Each time a child wishes to ask one of the above questions, he/she must take the appropripate card and ask you the question. This will combine reading with speaking practice and can also be used throughout the school day and not just during the English class.

● communication strategies: If you want children to use English as much as possible in the classroom, it is important that they learn a number of phrases to enable them to participate and maintain communication in English, for example: *Can you say that again, please? How do you say . . . in English, please? What does . . . mean, please? I don't understand! Can I have a . . ., please?*

By hearing this language over and over again, children learn to use it and soon realize that certain questions and requests can be made in English. Very often, pupils will tell other pupils to listen if they are chatting or to sit down if they are moving round! These phrases could also be written out in speech bubbles and stuck around the classroom.

Speaking practice
Speaking practice in the early stages of learning will mainly be
initiated by the teacher and will often consist of simple questions
and answers. However, many games provide pupils with opportunities to initiate conversation. These are described in more detail in
Chapter 14.

FEATURES
Below is a list of common activities which provide opportunities for
pupils to learn to speak in English. The features of these activities
include the following:

● Activity type
  Activities range from those which offer controlled practice to
  those offering communication practice. See Chapter 8 on learning English grammar and the lesson plan on pages 153–4
  which show how pupils move from a very controlled activity to
  one involving real communication.

● Fun
  Games, songs, rhymes, interviews, and so on provide a less
  formal context for practising English and often provide 'hidden'
  practice of specific language items. Memory skills are developed
  and the pupils are thus given chunks of language that they can
  take with them out of the classroom. Chapter 14 discusses the
  use of games, songs and rhymes in more detail.

● Interaction patterns
  It is important that interaction patterns in the classroom are
  varied as much as possible to avoid the situation where it is
  always the teacher who asks a question and the whole class
  who replies. Other interaction patterns include: teacher/indi-
  vidual pupil; individual pupil/teacher; pupil/pupil, for example,
  pupils speaking in turn in front of the class; whole class working
  in pairs or groups at the same time.

● Response
  Activities range from those which require a one word response
  to those requiring whole sentences or dialogues.

● Confidence building
  Activities should allow all pupils to participate according to
  their ability and stage of learning.

● Accuracy/Fluency
  Some activities should allow for practice in accuracy, others for
  fluency. It is important that children know which aspect an

activity is developing and why they are corrected more in activities focusing on accuracy than they are in those focusing on fluency.

● Amount of talking time

Each pupil in an average class of twenty-five pupils will have very little time to speak English if exercises are always done around the class, with each pupil saying one sentence. This would also become very boring. Pupils will have many more opportunities to practise speaking if opportunities are built into lessons for pupils to work together in pairs or groups. They then feel much more involved in a lesson and it helps them to learn to work together. For details on organizing pair and group work, see Chapter 11 on classroom management.

ACTIVITIES

The speaking activities shown in the chart (see Table 2) progress from those which provide tightly controlled practice to those which provide freer communication practice. See Chapter 8 on learning English grammar for a suggested procedure for presenting new structures.

Organizing speaking

Some of the activities described above require pupils to work together in pairs or groups or even to move around. Consideration will need to be given on how to arrange the classroom in order for these activities to be carried out smoothly. Chapter 11 describes this in more detail.

Pupils may also like to record themselves from time to time and listen to their recordings afterwards. For example, activities such as retelling a story could be recorded and played to pupils in other classes. Most pupils find this activity very motivating and it can help them become aware of the structures and vocabulary they are using and of certain aspects of English pronunciation, such as stress, rhythm and intonation, pace and voice variation. Ideally, a quiet area or corner in the classroom is needed for the recording to take place. This could be integrated into the 'listening corner', which is described in the section on learning to listen in this chapter.

Table 2 Speaking activities

Activity type	Purpose	Materials
1 Look, listen and repeat The teacher shows a picture, says the word and pupils repeat: *Look! An elephant. Repeat!* When the teacher is satisfied with her pupils' pronunciation, she can move on to another word. Once several new items have been introduced, the teacher can check by showing a picture and asking, *What's this?* and pupils reply.	● To introduce new vocabulary or structures ● The same technique, using a word card instead of a picture card will provide basic reading practice	Picture cards, for example, animals, food, colours, actions, clothes Word cards, as above
2 Listen and participate Examples of this are often found in storytelling sessions or when rhymes or poems are recited in class. Pupils are encouraged to participate by repeating key vocabulary and phrases.	● To involve pupils actively when listening to stories or rhymes ● To provide a meaningful and familiar context in which to repeat language items	Storybooks, rhymes, riddles, poems
3 Reading aloud Some games, like phonetic Bingo or Snap, require pupils to read words or sentences aloud.	● To practise pronunciation and sound/letter combinations	Bingo boards and cover cards Snap cards
4 Memory games Games like 'I went to market and bought . . .' and Chinese Whispers require children to repeat a certain structure or word.	● To develop memory skills ● To practise pronunciation ● To provide hidden pattern practice ● To improve concentration and listening skills	Short spoken messages or lists of items

Activity type	Purpose	Materials
5 Dramatization A story or situation can often be acted out, thereby involving pupils in a variety of different related activities such as learning lines, making costumes and props, making posters and invitations.	● To provide a memorable occasion for practising spoken English ● To develop confidence ● To develop memory skills ● To provide integrated skills practice	Storybooks Scripts (optional) Various materials for related activities
6 Rhymes, action rhymes, songs, chants These are learnt as chunks of language and involve pupils in imitating and miming. Rhymes or songs with actions also provide exercise and encourage body control.	● To develop memory skills ● To provide pronunciation practice ● To consolidate or introduce new language	Rhymes, songs, chants
7 Retelling a story This activity involves pupils in retelling a simplified version of a story. Children can often be helped in this activity with picture prompts, or by matching speech bubbles with pictures.	● To check if pupils have understood the main events in a story ● To provide pronunciation practice, as well as some storytelling techniques, such as disguising the voice, alternating pace and so on	Storybooks Captions written on cards or in speech bubbles, picture prompts

Activity type	Purpose	Materials
8 Look and ask This activity is often used to prepare pupils for freer activities such as pair work or questionnaires and surveys. The teacher can use a picture to prompt a pupil to ask a particular question. For example, the teacher gives a picture of three oranges to a pupil and instructs him or her to ask another pupil: *Benjamin, ask Mary!* Benjamin shows Mary the picture and asks, *How many oranges are there?* Mary replies. The teacher then asks the class. *Is that right?*	● To provide controlled practice were pupils are focusing on producing the correct grammatical form and pronunciation	Picture cards, for example, fruit, objects, clothes
9 Guessing games These types of games usually involve pupils in asking questions or describing something or someone. For example, pupils draw a picture of an animal or think of an animal they would like to have as a pet, without showing the class. The class must guess what it is: *Is it a cat?* and so on. Pupils can also describe someone in the class without saying his or her name: *She's got long hair. She's wearing a red pullover*, and so on, and the other pupils must listen and guess: *It's Sarah!*	● To provide a realistic context for practising the pronunciation of specific structures	None

Activity type	Purpose	Materials
10 Information gap These activities are usually carried out in pairs or groups and often involve pupils in asking and answering questions. One partner has some information that the other does not. The aim is to find out what this is in order to complete a task.	● To give pupils a chance to work independently of the teacher ● To practise fluency	Worksheets for pupils A and B (see page 121)
11 Questionnaires and surveys Pupils interview other classmates about, for example, their abilities, their likes and dislikes, and collate the information on a chart.	As above, and ● To practise listening skills ● To use the information collected for a specific purpose	Worksheets for pupils to complete. See Figure 3 on page 98
12 Roleplay Roleplay provides an opportunity for language that has been presented in one context to be used in another. For example, pupils could act out a shopping dialogue, making use of the 'shop corner'.	● To provide fluency practice ● To extend language use	Pupils may be given role cards, for example, Pupil A Pupil B _You want to buy eggs_ _You haven't got any eggs_ customer shop assistant

7   The written word

Learning to read in English

The initial stages

It is wise not to place too many reading demands on younger learners who are at an early stage of reading development. Children in many countries will have a working knowledge of the Roman alphabet, although children from countries with a different alphabet, such as India or Japan, will need to spend more time learning to form and recognize English letters. Early work on 'language awareness' can be carried out through activities such as noticing similarities and differences between alphabets, for example, the absence of accents for French speakers or tildes for Spanish speakers. It is also a good idea to encourage children to notice any examples of written English they may be able to find in their local environment. There may be signs, food labels or advertisements written in English which they could collect.

There is still a great deal of debate about the most effective methods for the teaching of reading. One method, known as phonics, which focuses on learning sound/letter correspondences to develop 'word attack' skills, remains popular with some primary school teachers. Recent research shows that exercises which focus exclusively on the development of phonic skills, where words are often decontextualized and have no purpose other than simply to practise sound/letter combinations, are not necessarily the best way of teaching reading. This is especially true of a language like English, which is not a phonetic language. Unlike languages such as Italian or Spanish, English has many confusing exceptions to sound/letter correspondences, especially with regard to vowels. Many reading experts stress the importance of helping learners to extract meaning from the written word so that they are not simply 'barking at print', that is, reading aloud with accuracy but with little or no real understanding. In practical terms, this means using activities to develop some useful phonic skills, such as consonant vowel combinations, and supplementing these with activities which emphasize the meaning and purpose of print.

Reading in English in the early stages will usually remain at the word level, where children play simple games such as Dominoes, Snap or Bingo to become familiar with typical letter combinations and to practise recognizing words. The learners at this stage will still need to rely on pictorial information to provide a context for understanding the written word. Other activities, such as labelling pictures or reading lists, help them to recognize key words in a written text. Gradually, the children will become more confident in reading the written word without other visual prompts.

Reading strategies

When children are listening to the spoken word they often use similar strategies to those used in understanding the written word. The section on listening described some of the successful strategies which can be used in the comprehension process, such as the importance of drawing upon previous knowledge about a topic or the usefulness of encouraging learners to use this knowledge by predicting what might be heard or read next. Research has shown that actively encouraging learners to use comprehension strategies such as these helps them understand both spoken and written passages more effectively. If learners know, for example, that they are listening to or reading something to get a general picture, they will listen or read in a slightly different way than if they are expected to listen or read in detail for specific parts of a spoken or written message. Another strategy for reading based on experience in listening involves working out the meaning of unfamiliar words from context, using pictures, general knowledge or 'intelligent guesswork' based on previous learning. For example, recognizing discourse markers such as *but* and *so* in spoken texts helps learners see a similar relationship between ideas in a written text.

Activities which include the use of charts provide an intermediate stage in reading development and also provide a framework to support children's listening and speaking skills. Reading practice may also be derived from listening work or may lead to writing. In this way, reading becomes integrated with other language skills.

The most common reading activities in many primary classrooms are gap-filling and answering traditional comprehension questions. Because they are so widely used and familiar to teachers, they are not referred to in this section. The chart (see Table 3) describes other kinds of reading activity which can be used with young learners. They range from activities which develop phonic skills or encourage sight recognition of key vocabulary to those which lead to practice in other skills, such as speaking, listening or writing. Many of these activities emphasize reading for meaning and reading to develop conceptual development or thinking skills, such as problem-solving. They are useful alternative techniques for checking reading comprehension and provide variety, thus helping to maintain the pupils' interest in reading.

Table 3 Reading activities

Activity type	Purpose	Materials
1 **Playing games such as Dominoes, Bingo and Snap** The children learn to match words, pictures or letters.	● To develop phonic skills and sight recognition of upper and lower case letters and common words	Domino cards Written words on cards for Snap, Bingo boards
2 **Playing games such as Odd-one-out or Spot the difference** Pupils identify similarities and differences between letters or words.	● To develop phonic skills and sight recognition of words	Flashcards or worksheets with words grouped in threes or fours
3 **Reading words and rearranging them to make sentences** A useful way of checking comprehension.	● For meaning ● To develop an understanding of word order	Sentences on cards cut up into individual words
4 **Matching or mapping two halves of a sentence so that they make sense**	● For meaning ● To become familiar with simple sentence patterns	Written parts of a sentence on card or a worksheet
5 **Using vocabulary prompt cards to make statements** The use of pictures prompts rehearses sentence patterns such as *I can skate/swim*, etc.	● As a prompt for speaking and pronunciation practice ● To become familiar with sentence patterns	Prompt cards with words and/or pictures showing, for example, nouns or action verbs

Activity type	Purpose	Materials
6 **Reading and ticking a chart to make sentences or ask questions** This also provides rehearsal of specific structures.	● As a prompt for interaction in pairs ● To rehearse sentence patterns and pronunciation	Chart on the blackboard or on a worksheet
7 **Matching pictures to speech bubbles** As the children listen to the teacher or a cassette, they read a selection of speech bubbles and choose the correct one.	● To reinforce listening skills ● To develop faster reading	Pictures and speech bubbles on card or on a worksheet
8 **Sequencing** While the children listen to a stretch of narrative or a description, they arrange sentences in the right order.	● For meaning, which acts as a useful context for discussion in pairs or groups ● For checking comprehension	Sentences written on card or sentences with boxes which are numbered to show their order
9 **Checking written statements** The children read statements, for example, riddles or sentences based on a survey, and check whether they are true or false, or write answers to the riddles.	● For meaning, to reinforce concepts ● For encouraging problem-solving	Written sentences on the blackboard or pinned next to a large graph or chart of a class survey
10 **Reading lists of words or different text types** For example, food packets, adverts, and classifying these under headings	● For meaning, to develop concepts ● To encourage problem-solving	Worksheets with lists of words and headings, for example: clothes for warm weather/clothes for cold weather

Organizing reading

Some of the activities described in the chart can be used with the whole class, while others can be done individually, in pairs or in groups. If different children are working on different activities, the activities will need to be kept in separate folders. These must be clearly labelled and/or colour-coded to show their level of difficulty so that the children can organize themselves and work independently. More details about classroom management can be found in Chapter 11.

Another good idea is to set up a reading display of different text types, both in the pupils' mother tongue and in English. These might include menus, timetables, stories, letters, advertisements, food packets, tickets, invitations, and so on. The class can then discuss different purposes for reading, for example, to find your way, to learn how to make something, to find information, to answer a question you have, to enjoy yourself, and so on. This kind of reading awareness has useful spin-offs, both for English and for the pupils' mother tongue.

One of the most obvious ways of linking the reading children do at home and at school is to use stories. More details about using stories and setting up a book corner to promote reading skills can be found in Chapter 13 and in Ellis and Brewster (1991).

Learning to write in English

The initial stages

Young children learning to write are coping with several features of the writing process: handwriting, spelling, punctuation, layout, the selection of the right vocabulary and grammar, as well as having and organizing ideas. This is difficult enough for children to do in the mother tongue but is even more so in a foreign language. Teachers need, therefore, to be especially sensitive to the different writing demands they are making on their pupils in English classes and to be aware of a variety of ways of supporting their writing. Much of the writing produced by children is clearly an opportunity to provide specific language practice, in selecting and spelling words correctly, as well as in using grammatical structures accurately. To do this, young learners often spend a lot of time completing tightly controlled written exercises to practise their English. Sometimes they may be encouraged to produce 'creative' or 'free' writing in English; this is particularly difficult and requires a great deal of support at word, sentence and text level.

In the early stages of learning English, the pupils will generally write very little. They are most likely to be engaged in some form of guided copying to produce words or sentences. It is a good idea to use copying in a way which encourages pupils to think; this means using crosswords, or anagrams, and matching, sequencing or classifying activities. Copying at word or sentence level can be guided through the use of support frameworks such as pictures, written models, tickcharts, flowcharts, and so on. These support frameworks give learners guidance on producing written work within clearly defined constraints. The use of a tickchart showing likes and dislikes, for example, can provide a simple sentence pattern such as *Jacques likes hot dogs but Louise likes sandwiches*. This sentence pattern, using the simple present tense and *but* to compare two pieces of information, can be adapted according to the information on the chart. Other types of guided copying are sometimes used to enable children to learn new vocabulary, group new words into word families, make lists of opposites, and generally consolidate word meanings. Lists of words can be provided for children to classify under different headings, such as words to do with meals, words for things to eat food with, shops where we buy food. The chart on page 78 (Table 4) describes some activities for practising writing words and sentences.

English spelling
Children will often find English spelling illogical and difficult. A technique which your pupils can use to learn new spellings is:

1 **Look:** notice letter shape and the number of letters, make a mental picture.
2 **Cover:** say the letters out loud, write the word in the air with one finger.
3 **Write:** write the word on paper.
4 **Check:** see if the spelling is correct; if not, repeat stages 1–4.

There are many useful spelling games you can play with younger learners. Here are four examples, some of which can be played with the whole class or groups to consolidate learning. Others are useful for remedial work in pairs or groups.

Hide and seek

Materials: Flashcards with selected words

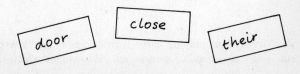

Method: Choose one child to stick six (or more) of the words on the blackboard using Blutack. The class close their eyes while one card is removed. The pupils then try to write down the missing word.

Table 4 Writing activities

Guided writing at word level

PURPOSE
To practise handwriting and spelling, and to learn new vocabulary
  1 making lists
  2 making personal dictionaries
  3 working out anagrams
  4 completing crosswords
  5 matching labels to pictures or diagrams
  6 classifying words under headings

Guided writing at sentence level

PURPOSE
To practise handwriting, spelling, and punctuation, and to learn new vocabulary and structures
  7 writing captions for pictures
  8 writing speech bubbles for cartoons or characters in a story
  9 writing sentences based on completed charts, e.g. surveys or questionnaires
 10 matching halves of sentences and copying
 11 sequencing sentences and copying
 12 correcting mistakes in written sentences
 13 answering questions

After practice with the whole class, this can be played in groups of two to eight. More than one card can be removed when the pupils are familiar with the game.

Snap

Materials: twenty-four playing cards with common words written on them. The words need to be grouped into families which have two or three letters in common, for example, *at*, *hat*, *mat*, *cat*; *the*, *other*, *mother*, *another*.

Method: The cards are divided equally between two players. Each player places the card face down in the usual way. When a player says 'Snap!', s/he has to say why the two cards are linked. No single letter matching is allowed. The winner is the first player to collect all of the cards.

Noughts and crosses

Materials: A traditional noughts and crosses board divided into nine squares. Noughts and crosses cards to cover the squares. A set of flashcards.

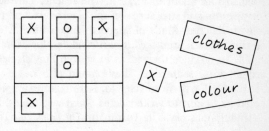

Method: Each player should have a set of cards showing some words which s/he finds difficult. This is given to the other player. The first player chooses a spelling from the list, shows it to his/her partner and lays it face down on the table. The second player then tries to write down the spelling. If it is correct, s/he can cover one square on the noughts and crosses board. The game continues until one player has made a horizontal, vertical or diagonal line on the board.

Word creation

Materials: A long word written on the blackboard. An outline of the shape represented by the word, for example, rhinoceros.

Method: Give the class a long word and ask them to make as many words as possible. To make the activity more appealing, use the outline shape of a rhinoceros to write in the words. Possible words are *chin*, *her*, *us*, *rice*, *score*, *hen*, etc.

Teaching writing

When developing children's writing skills, the teacher should help to make writing purposeful and contextualized wherever possible. This implies that the children should know why they are writing and that the writing they do has different purposes. Writing activities may be chosen to help them to spell, to use specific structural patterns to form sentences, or to practise freer writing that another pupil will read. It is important, therefore, that teachers provide a variety of writing activities, which range from controlled practice to guided or free practice, with these different purposes in mind. If writing is always strictly controlled, with children usually completing rather mechanical exercises, such as 'gap-filling', they will tend to lose interest in writing.

Practice in writing should always be preceded by specific activities, including the technique of 'modelling', which provides for the rehearsal of key vocabulary and structures. This means that children should not be asked to write something which they have not yet learned to talk about in English. The teacher can do this by putting key words and structures on the blackboard and providing children with different kinds of support frameworks, as described earlier. If the children are asked to write riddles, for example, they must be able to produce their ideas in spoken English before they are asked to write sentences. They should also have a written version available for them to refer to. Here is an example of how pupils could be taught to write riddles about vegetables, based on Tolstoy's traditional story 'The Turnip' (in *The Fairy Tale Treasury*).

Writing riddles about vegetables

1 Teach key vocabulary and structures.
   ● Teach/Revise names of vegetables, parts of plants, and adjectives to describe colour.
   ● Teach/Revise patterns such as *This is an orange vegetable . . . Do we eat the leaves of a carrot? Yes, we do. / No, we don't. We eat the root of a carrot but not the leaves.*

2 Provide a support framework.
   ● Put a tickchart or matrix on the blackboard and complete it with the whole class in a question and answer session.

EXAMPLE 1
Tickchart

	root	leaves	pod	seeds
lettuce	✗	✓	✗	✗
turnip	✓	✗	✗	✗
spinach	✗	✓	✗	✗
carrot	✓	✗	✗	✗
tomato	✗	✗	✗	✓

Do we eat the leaves of a turnip?
Yes, we do. / No, we don't.

3 Provide spoken practice in pairs.
  ● Using the same chart or matrix, ask the children to practise asking and answering questions in pairs, using the models above.

EXAMPLE 2
Matrix

	orange	red	yellow	green
root	carrot	—	turnip	—
leaves	—	—	—	spinach
pod	—	—	—	peas
cob	—	—	sweetcorn	—
seeds	—	tomato	—	—

This is an orange vegetable. We eat the root but not the leaves.

4 Provide a written model.
  ● Write these models on the blackboard:

  Riddle: *This vegetable is green. We eat the leaves but not the root. What is it?*
  Response: *Is it a lettuce?*
  Response: Yes, it is. / No, it isn't.

5 Provide written practice in pairs.
  ● Now ask the children to write riddles which will be given to another child to read and answer. Some pupils might like to copy the chart and add some different vegetables (write the spelling of these new vegetables on the blackboard).

6 Check written work produced.
  ● As the pairs are monitored, check that their spelling, word order, and sentence patterns are correct. Note any errors and provide feedback to individual pupils or to the whole class.

Writing in the later stages
It is useful to bear in mind that, as with stage four in riddles, writing to communicate is also an important aspect of the writing process. With this dimension in mind, it becomes increasingly important for teachers to create opportunities for older children to

do this. After two years of English, many pupils will have mastered some of the more basic skills in writing and should be encouraged to produce writing for a specific context and audience which goes beyond the practice stage. Now the teacher can encourage the older child to experiment with different text types, such as writing cards, letters, invitations, menus, or stories which another pupil might read. This implies that teachers should be aware of the differing writing demands text types make in terms of vocabulary, sentence structures, the organization of ideas, and layout. An important part of this process is collaboration between children during which they discuss ideas, plan the writing, and revise their work to produce a polished product. Some of this may, of course, need to take place in the mother tongue. Developing a sense of audience in order to communicate with someone else is possible even at a relatively early stage of learning English, as demonstrated in the example of writing riddles.

More creative writing activities, which encourage the children to compose their own sentences or texts, provide useful and motivating practice in planning, organizing ideas and under-standing the conventions of different text types, such as layout. Designing a seed packet, invitation, or advertisement, for example, requires a child to focus on the most important pieces of informa-tion and present them in a way which is eye-catching yet clear.

All of these activities are necessary and build upon one another; it is unrealistic to imagine that one can encourage creativity without specific skills practice at word or sentence level. Equally, it would be rather boring for all writing to remain at the practice level. To develop a greater awareness of different text types, the children should ideally have collected, discussed, and read a variety of text types, perhaps in both the mother tongue and in English. The texts which the pupils choose to write in the English class will probably be linked to a topic or story which they have been doing. Some common text types which can be used are listed on page 83. Others which have been found useful can probably be added too.

Some schools may have a computer which enables the pupils to practise word-processing. This is particularly motivating for chil-dren as it makes editing easy and produces a very polished product. The computer may also have some programs designed to help children with specific skills, such as spelling.

In order to make pupils' work more public and more motivating, they can be asked to produce some of the writing exercises, such as writing sentences and cutting them in half, for other children to match. They can also be asked to practise handwriting by making

Poems/Stories	Descriptions
Shape poems	Tickets
Alphabet poems	Diaries
Cartoons	Riddles
Collaborative stories	Seed packets
Newspapers/Magazines	Food packets
Simple autobiographies	Advertisements
Passports	Posters
Plays/Dialogues	Invitations
	Tickets
	Descriptive letters
	Maps or plans + descriptions

Lists/Charts	Instructions
Shopping lists	How to play a game
Menus	Recipes
Things to take on holiday	How to make a model
Favourite sports	Letters with written directions
Famous people from	Messages
different countries	Notices

some of the flashcards or speech bubbles used in the spelling games or other activities. It is important, in all cases, to display the children's written work occasionally, as this helps to maintain interest and can also encourage pupils to raise their standards! For more ideas on display, see Chapter 11.

Although many of the activities in this chapter have been described under separate headings, it can be seen how they usually link with other skills. For example, a reading activity can be based on listening, which in turn can lead on to a writing activity. This integration of skills is important, especially as the pupils make progress and become more confident in using English.

References and further reading

Briggs, R. and V. Haviland, 1974. *The Fairy Tale Treasury*: Puffin.

Brumfit, C., Moon, J. and Tongues, R. (Eds.), 1991. *Teaching English to Children*: Harper-Collins.

Dunn, O., 1983. *Beginning English with Children*: Macmillan.

Dunn, O., 1984. *Developing English with Young Learners*: Macmillan.

Ellis, G. and J. Brewster, 1991. *The Storytelling Handbook for Primary Teachers*: Penguin English.

Halliwell, S., 1992. *Teaching English in the Primary Classroom*: Longman.

Holmes, B., 1991. *Communication re-activated, Pathfinder 6*: CILT.

Jones, B., 1992. *Being Creative, Pathfinder 10*: CILT.

Kennedy, C. and J. Jarvis, 1991. Ideas and Issues in Primary ELT: Nelson.

8   Sounds, words and structures

Learning the pronunciation of English

There are bound to be some differences in pronunciation between the pupils' mother tongue and English. Children are generally good at imitating and will 'pick up' your model of pronunciation more easily than adults. Some remedial work may be needed, but usually pronunciation teaching forms an integral part of your presentation of new words and sentence patterns and subsequent practice activities. The need to provide a good model of pronunciation in these early stages is therefore of great importance.

Songs and rhymes will be particularly useful for the teacher in developing the pupils' awareness of how English sounds (for further details about this, see Chapter 14). Careful consideration needs to be given to recent views of pronunciation which discourage the use of 'pronunciation drills', especially those which contrast words with different sounds. Generally speaking, these are not appropriate for young learners: the children become easily bored because this type of practice is meaningless and de-contextualized. Many practice activities, such as making surveys using Yes/No questions, or games, will, more naturally, involve repetition, which creates 'hidden' opportunities for pronunciation practice but which are more meaningful and contextualized.

A brief summary of the main areas of pronunciation difficulties which teachers need to know about is given below.

Individual sounds

There may be some consonant sounds which are not present in the mother tongue but which occur in English. These will not necessarily cause problems, although some may be more difficult to master than others. One example is /ð/, which occurs in English but not in French. In cases like this, it will be useful to demonstrate how these sounds are made by showing what should be happening to the lips, tongue, and teeth.

The pronunciation of vowels is more likely to cause problems; again the teacher needs to demonstrate the way in which these sounds are made, for example, whether the mouth is quite open or closed, and whether the lips are rounded or spread out. Try, wherever possible, to demonstrate the word on its own first of all, but move quickly to putting it in a sentence so that pronunciation practice is more meaningful. It may be necessary to spend a little time making the children aware of the differences between /ɪ/and

/iː/, for example, using the technique of 'ear-training'. Children may find it difficult to tell the difference between two sounds if they cannot, first of all, hear that the sounds are actually different. Listening exercises and games where the children learn to hear these differences can include listening for sounds which are the same or different, or by spotting the 'odd man out' in a series. Phonetic Bingo, which is played in the same way as ordinary Bingo, but which includes items with easily confused sounds, is a useful game to play to practise sound discrimination.

Sounds in connected speech

It is important that pronunciation teaching does not concentrate entirely on the production of individual sounds. Practising how sounds blend together in informal speech is equally important. One of the pronunciation features present in English is 'linking' where certain sounds are run on together to avoid a jerky, staccato effect. This happens most commonly where a word ending in a consonant or a vowel is followed by a word beginning with a vowel. Four examples can be seen in the following action rhyme:

Chop, chop, choppity-chop.

Cut off the bottom,

And cut off the top.

What there is left we will

Put in the pot:

Chop, chop, choppity-chop.

Linking the words in this way helps to keep the smooth flow of English. This rhyme is also useful for practising the consonant /tʃ/ and the short vowels /ɒ/ /ʌ/and /ɪ/.

Stress and rhythm

English is a 'stress-timed' language, which means that stressed beats occur at roughly equal intervals of time, regardless of how many syllables there are between each beat. A useful way of demonstrating this is to ask the children to clap to the strong beats, while adding more and more syllables between the claps (strong beats are in capital letters):

ONE		TWO		THREE		FOUR
ONE	and	TWO	and	THREE	and	FOUR
ONE	and a	TWO	and a	THREE	and a	FOUR
ONE and then a TWO and then a THREE and then a FOUR						

Songs, rhymes and jazz chants are an excellent illustration of the way in which stress and rhythm work in English. Again, the children can be asked to clap the rhythm.

Words which tend to be stressed are important 'content' words which give the main part of a message. These words include nouns, verbs, adjectives, and adverbs. When a word is stressed, three things tend to happen:

1 the stressed word sounds slightly louder than the others;
2 the vowel in the stressed word is clearly pronounced; and so
3 tends to sound longer.

Try to notice this with the two rhymes above. What also happens is that the words which do not have stress often have to be said rather quickly to fit them in. This means that they are shorter and the vowel sounds are not pronounced as clearly. In fact, these vowels often change to an easily pronounced vowel, such as /ə/; /ɪ/ and /ʊ/. Words which do not receive strong stress are referred to as 'weak forms'. These occur most commonly with 'grammatical' words in a sentence, such as the articles, auxiliary or verbs or modals, and pronouns or prepositions, when they are not a very important part of the message. Weak forms in the rhyme given on page 86 are *the*, *and*, *we*, which are pronounced /ðə/; /ən/; /wɪ/.

Intonation

Some of the most important functions of intonation in English are to help emphasize the most strongly stressed word in a sentence; to show the grammatical function of what is being said, for example, whether something is a statement or question; and to show feelings and emotions. The most usual intonation pattern in English uses a falling tone. This is used to make:

● a short statement.

For example: *'Here is a house.'*

● questions with words such as *who*, *what*, *why*, etc.

For example: *'Where's the pencil?'*

● commands.

For example: 'Cut off the bottom.'

● exclamations to show surprise, anger or give a warning.

For example: 'Look out!'

The rising tone is used:

● to make requests.

For example: 'Can we come too?'

● to make questions from statements.

For example: 'He's going out?'

● in Yes/No questions.

For example: 'Would you like a sweet?'

● in clauses or phrases that come before the main clause in the sentence.

For example: 'What there is left we will put in the pot.'

Improving your own pronunciation

If you have any published material on cassette, listen to it carefully and notice some of the features referred to above. You might like to think about the following questions after you have listened to a short pre-recorded dialogue or rhyme.

● Are there any individual sounds which you (or your pupils) find particularly difficult?
● Are there any examples of linking?
● Is the sentence stressed in the way you would expect?
● Are there any examples of weak forms?
● How many examples of falling or rising tones can you hear?

Where you have special difficulties, you can practise repeating particular phrases using the model provided by the cassette. It is also useful to listen to as much authentic English as possible, such as radio broadcasts or television. You might like to record yourself speaking and note your main strengths and weaknesses in pronunciation. If you choose one area at a time to concentrate on, you should gradually build up your confidence and develop both accuracy and fluency. See Chapter 16 for further details on how to do this.

Learning English vocabulary

This section looks at the different ways in which new vocabulary can be introduced, activities for practising and checking vocabulary, and activities for consolidating vocabulary.

In the early stages of language learning, it is important to decide which vocabulary items you will want your pupils to produce and which you will want them to recognize only. This will depend, of course, on the language learning materials you are using. Most will include basic vocabulary essential for communication as well as special interest or child-centred words. Special interest words include those which are of special interest to children but may not immediately be on the tip of your tongue! Can you, for example, write down five words related to the following topics?

	Witches	Dinosaurs	Circus	Fairground	Toys
1	_____	_____	_____	_____	_____
2	_____	_____	_____	_____	_____
3	_____	_____	_____	_____	_____
4	_____	_____	_____	_____	_____
5	_____	_____	_____	_____	_____

Some child-centred vocabulary may be unfamiliar to you in English but will most probably be the kind of vocabulary your pupils will want to learn and find the easiest to learn and remember. You may need to equip yourself with a good dictionary (see the Appendix).

Introducing new vocabulary

When introducing vocabulary, it should ideally be presented in a context which is familiar to the child. Visual support is very important to help convey meaning and to help pupils memorize new words. The sections on learning to listen and reading emphasize the importance of pupils working out the meaning of unknown words when listening to spoken English or when reading. The activities described below can provide an initial stage which helps pupils develop an awareness of clues as aids to meaning, such as illustrations, similarity to a word in their own language, the context, and so on.

Research has shown that words are often remembered in groups which have something in common. Because of this, try to introduce new words in:

● lexical sets, for example, shops, fruit, rooms in a house

- rhyming sets, for example, *pat, bat, rat, hat*
- colour sets, grouping together things that are green, for example, *a pea, a leaf, an apple, a caterpillar, a bird*
- grammatical sets, for example, adjectives, verbs, prepositions, nouns.

Grouping words together in this way can help pupils associate new words with words they already know and can aid retention and recall.

Whenever possible, get pupils to use their senses: hearing, seeing, tasting, smelling, and touching, to help memorize words and understand their meanings. For example, pupils could find something cold or hot in the classroom and touch this, and so on.

Teachers often ask how many new words it is possible to introduce per lesson. Although there is no definitive answer, it is probably wise not to introduce more than ten. The number of new words that can be introduced in one lesson will depend on factors such as the linguistic and conceptual level of your pupils, the similarity of the words to the mother tongue, how rich and memorable the context is in which the words are presented, how easy it is to illustrate meaning, and so on. It should also be remembered that some children cannot rely solely on a word being presented orally. Many need written reinforcement and will, therefore, like to see the written form of the word in order to aid retention. However, do not write the word on the board until you have practised its pronunciation first.

Here are some techniques that can be used to introduce new vocabulary:

USING OBJECTS
Much of the vocabulary at this stage of children's learning will consist of concrete nouns. This means that there are plenty of objects that can be used to show meanings. Objects in the classroom can be used or things brought to the classroom. Introducing a new word by showing the real object often helps pupils to memorize the word through visualization.

DRAWING
Objects can either be drawn on the blackboard or drawn on flash cards. The latter can be used again and again in different contexts if they are made with card and covered in plastic.

USING ILLUSTRATIONS AND PICTURES
A great deal of vocabulary can be introduced by using illustrations or pictures, either those found in the language learning materials you are using or by making your own visual aids, using pictures

from magazines and so on. Visual support helps pupils understand the meaning and helps to make the word more memorable.

MIME, EXPRESSIONS AND GESTURES

Many words can be introduced through mime, expressions, and gestures. For example, adjectives: *sad*, *happy*; nouns: mime taking a hat off your head to teach *hat* and so on.

USING OPPOSITES

This technique allows pupils to associate words with a concept they already understand in their mother tongue and often pupils will learn two words instead of one. For example, *long/short*, *big/little*, *straight/curly*, *town/country*, *ill/well*, and so on. Meanings can also be conveyed using simple line drawings.

GUESSING FROM COMTEXT

Encourage pupils to take risks and guess the meanings of words they don't know as much as possible. This will help them build up their self-confidence so that they can work out the meanings of words when they are on their own. There are many clues pupils can use to establish meanings for themselves:

● illustrations
● similarity of spelling or sound in the mother tongue
● general knowledge.

ELICITING

Once a context is established, you can ask pupils (you may need to do this in the mother tongue) what words they would expect to find or what they would expect someone to say or do in a particular situation. For example, you may want to introduce vocabulary related to witches and their spells. If you ask pupils what ingredients they think a witch may put in a spell, they will suggest all types of things: *a worm*, *a bat*, *a spider*, *a lizard*, and so on. Even if pupils suggest these words in their mother tongue, it shows they are thinking in the appropriate semantic area. This provides you with the ideal opportunity to introduce the word in English as the desire to know it has come from the pupils them-selves. This technique is far more motivating and memorable than simply giving pupils a list of words to learn.

TRANSLATION

If none of the above techniques work, translate. There are always some words that need to be translated and this technique can save a lot of time.

When using any of the above techniques, the following procedure can be used. Illustrate the word in one of the ways above. If a child knows the word, ask him or her to say it and, if it is correct, use this as your model. If not, say the word yourself. Ask the class to repeat. Check pronunciation. Say it again if necessary. Ask individual pupils to repeat the word and then the whole class again. You may then want to write the word on the board.

Practising and checking vocabulary

Once a new word has been introduced, you will want to provide opportunities for pupils to practise it and check that they understand it. There are a variety of activities you can use to do this.

WHAT'S MISSING?

This game can be played by using illustrations drawn by yourself, or reproduced from the language materials you are using, and stuck on the board, or drawn or written directly on the board. The number of items you include will depend on the level of your pupils, but you may need to limit this to a maximum of ten. Ask pupils to close their eyes. Remove an item from the board. Pupils open their eyes and tell you what is missing. You could ask the rest of the class, *Is he/she right?*

The game can also be played as a team game. Divide the class into two teams. Play as above, each team taking a turn. Each time a pupil is correct, he/she wins a point for their team.

KIM'S GAME

This works in the same way as above but, traditionally, objects are used and displayed on a tray or a table.

MATCHING WORDS TO PICTURES

Pupils match words to the corresponding picture. Words and pictures are jumbled up on the board and pupils match them.

GUESSING GAMES

Hide and Seek A pupil goes outside the classroom while the others hide an object or an animal. The child comes back and must guess where it is: *Is it under the table?* and so on. This practises prepositions and nouns.

Mime A pupil mimes, for example, an animal or a profession, and the class must guess what it is/who they are: *Is it a . . .?, Are you a . . .?*

GIVING INSTRUCTIONS/PICTURE DICTATION

The teacher gives instructions, focusing on specific vocabulary. For example, colours and shapes: *Show me a red square*; colours and numbers: *Colour number 4 red*; objects: *Show me a table, Draw a table, Touch a table*, and so on.

SEQUENCING
Jumble up pictures on the board. The teacher or a pupil gives instructions: *Put the chocolate cake first* and so on.

LABELLING
Pupils label a picture in order to practise different nouns from lexical sets. For example, labelling different parts of the body or different rooms in a house.

BINGO
Bingo can take various forms. The board can consist of words or pictures. As words are called out, pupils put down picture or word cover cards. This can involve pupils in matching the spoken form of the word with its pictorial or written form.

CLASSIFYING/SORTING
Pupils sort words into different categories. For example, hot and cold things, sweet or salty foods, red things, and so on.

DOMINOES
Here children practise reading and matching words which rhyme.

WORD STARS
Pupils arrange words which rhyme on a star diagram. This organization provides a rich and visual contextualization. If pupils keep a vocabulary book or picture dictionary, words could also be organized in this way in them. See below.

MEMORY GAMES
Chinese Whispers Give one pupil in a group or team a list of words or a word in a sentence which they must remember and whisper to the next child. This child whispers to the next child and so on until the last child is reached. This child must compare the list with the first list and see if it has changed.
Market Game A child begins, *I went to market and bought a pie*. The next child adds an item, *I went to market and bought a pie and a bun*, and so on.

Remembering Details from a Story Stories provide a rich and memorable context in which to learn vocabulary. For example, in *The Very Hungry Caterpillar*, pupils remember the different sorts of fruit the caterpillar ate and work out how many things the caterpillar ate through. In *Spot's Birthday Party*, pupils remember which animals hid where and match a picture of the animal to a picture of the hiding place.

WORD MACHINES

These can be used to help children develop a working knowledge of possible letter combinations and helps with spelling. The machine changes a word by performing one (or more) operations on it to form a new word.

There are, of course, many other activities that can be used to practise vocabulary and you may like to devise some of these yourself, for example, crosswords, hangman, odd word out, or card games such as Snap and Happy Families, I-spy, and so on.

Consolidating vocabulary

Many children learn new words relatively quickly but they also forget them quickly too. Once new vocabulary has been introduced and practised, pupils should be encouraged to devise techniques they can use on their own to consolidate and revise the words. Many language learning materials recycle words showing how they can be used in different contexts. This provides an ideal opportunity for revision and the introduction of new words from the same lexical set. What can pupils do with words as they learn them? Many ask to write them down as this aids retention. Here are some techniques you can propose to your pupils which will allow them to build up their own personalized vocabulary learning strategies.

PICTURE DICTIONARIES/VOCABULARY BOOKS

Encourage pupils to create their own picture dictionaries or vocabulary books. Discuss ways of organizing these, for example, alphabetically or by topic. It is useful for pupils to use a ring folder for this purpose so that they can add new pages when necessary. Pupils collect or draw pictures to illustrate the meaning of a word. They can write the word in English too. Some may want to write the word in their own language. Do not stop children doing this as for some it can be a useful learning strategy.

A class dictionary can also be made in the same way and hung on the classroom wall.

It is a good idea to have a dictionary for classroom use which will enable pupils to find out the meaning of new words themselves and help them develop useful study skills. This could be a picture dictionary (see, for example, the *Puffin First Picture Dictionary*), a bilingual dictionary, or an elementary monolingual dictionary.

WORD FAMILIES/SETS

Encourage pupils to build up their own word sets as an alternative to a picture dictionary. Pictures can be copied from stories or cut out from magazines, coloured and labelled, and kept in envelopes, by topic. Each envelope can be labelled, for example, *clothes*, *fruit*, *toys*, and so on.

VOCABULARY CARDS

Pupils can make their own sets of vocabulary cards for self-testing. Discuss ways of conveying meaning, for example, a picture, translation, or putting the word in a sentence. On one side of the card pupils draw, for example, a picture and on the other they write the word in English. They pick up a card, look at the picture, and try to recall the word in English. They can then turn over the card and check if they are correct.

COLLAGES

Making collages is a useful way of revising vocabulary. Pupils collect pictures around a particular theme, for example, animals, clothes, dinosaurs, and stick these on to a large sheet of paper. These can be used to decorate the classroom and can be added to on an on-going basis.

RESEARCHING

Encourage pupils to look for similarities between English words and words in their own language and to build up a wall display or collage. Alternatively, they may like to look for English words that are used in their country on food packets, in clothes, in the street, and so on, which will provide a language awareness activity.

Learning English Grammar

The formal teaching of grammar is not usually a major objective when teaching English to children. We saw in Chapter 4 that there has been a move away from seeing language learning solely as the learning and practising of new vocabulary and grammatical forms to learning English for communication purposes. However, the learning of English grammar and basic sentence patterns is nevertheless important to enable children to participate in activities which focus on purposeful communication. Chapter 4 also emphasizes the importance of relating language learning to children's experience in everyday life. One way of doing this is to use topics or themes as your starting point so that the language and the language learning activities arise naturally from the topic. Another way is to use stories, which can introduce pupils to the grammatical patterns of English in a natural and authentic way. The rich context helps them understand the meanings they convey. Furthermore, as children enjoy listening to stories over and over again, this allows certain structures to be acquired without being formally or explicitly introduced. The natural repetition in some stories also encourages pupils to join in when the story is being told, thereby providing a type of pattern practice. Games, rhymes, and songs also provide practice of specific language patterns in a less formal way.

Appropriate language use requires a knowledge of both the form and the functions of a language. Children should therefore be provided with opportunities from an early stage to use grammatical structures for real communicative purposes. This will make language learning much more meaningful and motivating. For example, *Wh* questions can be used for asking for information in a pair work activity where one pupil has some information that the other needs in order to complete a task. The Learning to speak section in Chapter 6 describes many other activities which allow pupils to participate in real communication.

Presenting a structure

The following procedure for presenting a structure is one that is used frequently with young learners.

The example below is for presenting the structure *Do you like . . .?* / *Yes, I do.* / *No, I don't.*

PRESENTATION

1 Revise vocabulary for different food items.

2 Hold up a picture and ask: *Nicholas, do you like sausages?* He will probably reply *Yes* or *No* at this stage.

3 Using other pictures ask two or three other pupils the question. Now say: *Listen! Yes, I do. Repeat!* Whole class repeats. *Again!* Now ask individual pupils to repeat until you are satisfied with the pronunciation. Ask the question again and insist on the reply *Yes, I do.*

4 Introduce *No, I don't* by repeating this procedure.

5 Give a picture to a pupil and say: *Ask me*. The pupil may be able to produce the question *Do you like cherry pie?* or maybe not. If yes, ask him/her to repeat the question and get the class to repeat. If not, say the question yourself and encourage the class to repeat. Then ask individual pupils, as above.

6 Now give a picture to a pupil and instruct him/her to ask another pupil: *Nicholas, ask Sarah!* Nicholas asks: *Sarah, do you like ice-cream?* Sarah replies: *Yes, I do. / No, I don't.* Continue in this way until you are satisfied.

7 You may or may not wish to write the question and reply on the board.

CONTROLLED PRACTICE

8 Now take a picture but do not let your pupils see what it is. Invite them to ask *Do you like salami?* and so on until someone says the food item you have.

9 Pupils now play the above game in pairs.

PRODUCTION

10 Now distribute worksheets (see Figure 3). This activity involves pupils in an interview activity. They go round the class asking about their classmates' likes and dislikes. Monitor or join in the activity yourself. If you find pupils are having problems, make a note of what these are and revise them after the activity.

11 To round up the activity, pupils can collate the information they have collected on their worksheets.

This procedure allows a structure to be presented, practised and produced in a controlled framework, where pupils move from a situation carefully directed by the teacher to one where they use English for a genuine purpose and direct their own learning. It can also be successfully applied to teaching other structures. See the lesson plan in Chapter 12, where language for describing a person, *She's got . . ., She's wearing . . .,* is presented, practised and produced in a similar progression.

For further ideas on how to present, practise and produce structures, see the Learning to speak section in Chapter 6.

Do You Like....

	sausages	watermelon	chocolate cake	salami	cherry pie	pickles	cup cakes	lollipops	Swiss cheese	and ice-cream.
me	✓	✗	✓	✗	✓	✓	✓	✓	✗	✓
Jo	✓	✓	✓	✗	✓	✗	✓	✗	✓	✓
Sarah	✓	✗	✓	✓	✓	✗	✓	✓	✓	✓

Figure 3   Sample worksheet

Discovery grammar activities

Many pupils in Europe are well grounded in formal grammar in their own language and understand the metalanguage to describe it. Teachers of English can, therefore, capitalize on this by encouraging pupils to compare their own language with English and spot similarities and differences and attempt to work out the rules of English grammar for themselves. This approach turns grammar into a problem-solving activity where pupils consolidate knowledge of a structure that has been introduced as suggested above or establish the structure for themselves without an explanation from the teacher.

Here is an example of a discovery grammar activity which focuses on word order in English.

Pupils already know some adjectives of colour and vocabulary for clothes and can produce simple descriptions, such as, *his red pullover, his black boots,* and so on. Adjectives of size, *big, long, tall* are introduced as well as further vocabulary for clothes: *shoes, stockings, cloak* and *hat.*

Pupils listen to a description of a witch putting on the above clothes and must sequence the pictures below in the correct order.

She put on her black stockings, her big black shoes, her long black cloak and her tall black hat.

Meg ang Mog by Helen Nicoll and Jan Pieńkowski

Children are now asked the following questions, most likely in their mother tongue, to encourage them to reflect on word order in English and to make comparisons with their own language.

- Which words are adjectives?
- Which words are nouns?
- Where do adjectives go in English?

- Where do adjectives for colour go?
- Where do adjectives for size go?
- Where do they go in your language?

To provide further practice, the following words are written on cards and stuck on the board. Individual pupils come to the board and make a phrase by putting words in the correct order. For example, *Her long, black cloak.*

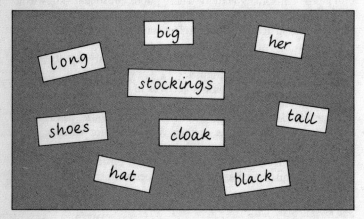

This activity shows how pupils are not given the rules or structures but are helped to work them out for themselves through discovery learning. The model descriptions provide the basis for discussion, comparison and hypothesis. The pupils are then provided with further examples to experiment with and to test out their 'rule'. This problem-solving approach helps pupils to develop their thinking capacity and build up their confidence. There are many other occasions when these activities could be used and you may like to devise activities yourself where appropriate.

References and further reading

Carle, E., 1974. *The Very Hungry Caterpillar*: Puffin.
Hill, E., 1985. *Spot's Birthday Party*: Puffin.
Thompson, B. and C. Berridge, 1988. *Puffin's First Picture Dictionary*: Puffin.

9 Learning to learn

Chapters 3 and 4 have discussed the importance of helping pupils learn how to learn. This chapter aims to provide some practical examples of how this important area can be developed.

The content of learning to learn

Learning to learn, also referred to as learner training by EFL/ESL teachers, is an umbrella term for a wide variety of activities designed to develop learning strategies. It is primarily concerned with the processes of learning and aims to focus pupils' attention on **how** they learn in addition to **what** they learn. It takes into account that different learners have different ways of learning and different preferences regarding activities and learning materials. It therefore aims to develop self-awareness and gradually lead pupils to a conscious development of their own learning strategies, so they can become more effective and independent learners. Many of these strategies can be applied to whatever subject a pupil is learning and, although difficult to isolate, can be broadly classified as follows:

- Metacognitive strategies. These include planning for learning, hypothesizing, self-assessment and monitoring and involve learners in reflecting on the learning process.

- Cognitive strategies. These include sorting, classifying, comparing, matching, predicting, developing an awareness of visual and audio clues as aids to meaning, repeating, using a class library or dictionary. They involve pupils in doing things with the language and their learning materials and relate to specific activities in specific skills areas such as listening for specific information, sorting words into groups and so on.

- Social mediation strategies. These include collaborating and peer-correction and involve pupils in co-operating together in language-learning activities. Opportunities for developing these are usually set up through pair or group work activities and project work.

Communication strategies which allow pupils to maintain communication in English and negotiate meaning are described in the Learning to speak section in Chapter 6.

The benefits of learning to learn

Although there have been few empirical studies to evaluate the effects of learning to learn in terms of performance, most teachers have observed increased motivation and a more questioning, active and personal involvement in their learners as justifiable outcomes. Developing curiosity and positive attitudes towards foreign language learning with young learners is particularly important. Most are learning a foreign language for the first time and early foreign language learning aims to provide them with a positive experience and the desire to continue. Early foreign language learning also aims to prepare pupils for the more formal and exam-orientated courses in secondary school. Learning to learn provides them with the basic learning tools for this.

The methodology of learning to learn

When focusing on learning to learn for young learners, for whom school and learning are central in their lives, it is particularly important that it is introduced in a meaningful learning context, in an overt and explicit way and strategies demonstrated with transfer in mind. This will help pupils to see how certain strategies can be used with different tasks or subjects. For example, a self-testing strategy using two-sided cards can be used for practising English vocabulary, times tables or countries and their capitals. In fact, virtually any class activity may be used for learning to learn. All that is necessary is to focus attention upon the learning process aspect of an experience, which always exists side by side with the content.

The lesson plan in Chapter 12 (see Figure 18) shows how the three types of strategies described above have been integrated into a lesson focusing on the language of description.

The teachers' role

The teacher plays an important role in helping children learn how to learn. Children can learn different strategies but they rarely use them spontaneously. With prompting from the teacher, they will gradually learn to use them independently. A teacher may well adopt an activity-based or enquiry-based approach actively to involve the children in the learning process. This provides concrete external cues for children and often involves practical demands in their performance. Teachers may also take on a questioning role, often using the learners' mother tongue, to encourage pupils to reflect on their basic assumptions about learning, as well as to model the types of questions about learning that pupils can gradually learn to ask themselves.

A further important role for the teacher is to share with her learners, in a way which is accessible to them, information about language and language learning. This would include making sure pupils are clear about the purpose of an activity as well as discussing different learning strategies and activities. It is also extremely important that a teacher creates a learning environment where pupils feel secure so they can experiment with the new language and build up the necessary self-confidence in order to take risks.

Below is a description of some of the strategies that can be developed in the English language classroom.

Metacognitive strategies

Problem-solving and hypothesizing
Pupils are encouraged to work out the rules of grammar for themselves. This can be done by looking at examples of the foreign language and working out why, for example, *a* or *an* is used in front of certain nouns; to reflect on the use of countable or uncountable nouns; or on word order in English. See the Section on Learning English grammar in Chapter 8 for an example of the latter.

Reviewing
Pupils can be taught to review systematically if they are asked at the beginning of each lesson: *What did we do last lesson?* or *What did you learn last lesson?* and, at the end of each lesson: *What did we do today?*, *What did you learn?* This type of reviewing is important as it clarifies work covered, helps pupils perceive progress, and helps them become aware of what they do and don't know so they can identify what to revise.

Self-questioning
Pupils can be taught how to ask themselves questions about their learning. For example, the teacher can question them about parts of the lesson they found easy or difficult and why; about activities they enjoyed or didn't enjoy and how they helped or didn't help them learn; about how they guessed the meaning of an unknown word; and so on. Through this form of interrogation, the teacher is modelling for the learner the type of questions they can eventually

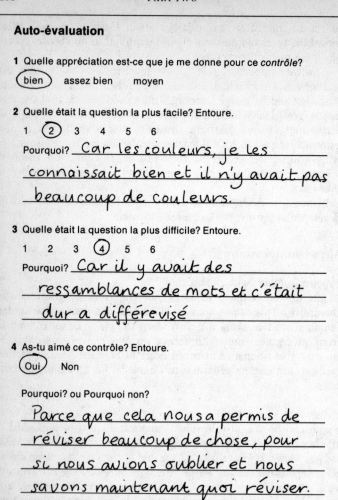

Auto-évaluation

1 Quelle appréciation est-ce que je me donne pour ce *contrôle*?

(bien)   assez bien   moyen

2 Quelle était la question la plus facile? Entoure.

1   (2)   3   4   5   6

Pourquoi? Car les couleurs, je les connaissait bien et il n'y avait pas beaucoup de couleurs.

3 Quelle était la question la plus difficile? Entoure.

1   2   3   (4)   5   6

Pourquoi? Car il y avait des ressamblances de mots et c'était dur a différevisé

4 As-tu aimé ce contrôle? Entoure.

(Oui)   Non

Pourquoi? ou Pourquoi non?

Parce que cela nous a permis de réviser beaucoup de chose, pour si nous avions oublier et nous savons maintenant quoi réviser.

Figure 4   Self-assessment questionnaire 1 (French)

ask themselves. This can also help them identify their strong and weak points and reach a greater understanding of why certain aspects of learning may be more difficult for them than others.

Self-assessment
Self-assessment is an important way of encouraging pupils to take on more responsibility for their own learning. The teacher can begin doing this by asking pupils questions as described above, for

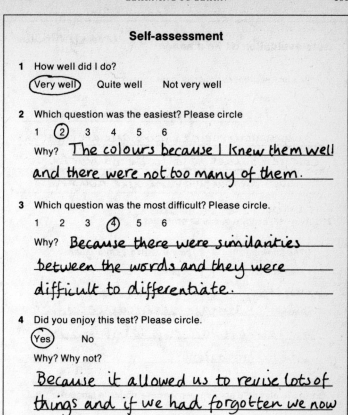

Self-assessment

1 How well did I do?

(Very well)   Quite well   Not very well

2 Which question was the easiest? Please circle

1 ② 3   4   5   6

Why? The colours because I knew them well
and there were not too many of them.

3 Which question was the most difficult? Please circle.

1   2   3   ④   5   6

Why? Because there were similarities
between the words and they were
difficult to differentiate.

4 Did you enjoy this test? Please circle.

(Yes)   No

Why? Why not?

Because it allowed us to revise lots of
things and if we had forgotten we now
knew what to revise.

Figure 4a   Self-assessment questionnaire 1 (English)

example, after an activity or a lesson or after a unit from a
coursebook has been completed or a storybook has been read, even
after a test! Pupils can be asked questions such as, *Did you enjoy
this unit/topic/story?, Why/Why not?, What did you learn?, How well
did you do?*, and so on. Pupils' comments can be recorded and
listened to afterwards. This type of discussion will probably take
place in the mother tongue but can be used to improve pupils' self-
expression. A lesson can also be video-recorded and viewed and
questions asked about pupils' participation in the lesson and so on.
Pupils could also record themselves carrying out a particular
activity in English, then listen and judge their performance. You

Auto-évaluation de fin d'année   Tuesday 19th June

1 As-tu aimé apprendre l'anglais cette année?

(Oui?)   Non?

Pourquoi? _Je voulais apprendre une autre_
langue pour ne pas faire que du français
car je voulais déjà la découvrir la
langue anglaise avant que nous ne
fasions de l'anglais.

2 Quelle est l'histoire que tu as préférée?

☐ The Snowman   ☐ The Very Hungry Caterpillar

☐ Meg and Mog   ☐ Pat the Cat

☒ Meg's Eggs

Pourquoi? _J'aimais beaucoup cette histoire_
car j'aime beaucoup les animaux
préhistorique.

3 Quelle(s) activité(s) ou exercices (dans la liste ci-dessous) as-tu
trouvé le plus utile pour apprendre cette nouvelle langue?

☐ dictées d'images   ☒ réflexion sur la langue

☒ dictée de l'heure   ☐ contrôles

☐ classification   ☐ théâtre

☐ questions/réponses   ☐ dessin

☐ questionnaires/enquêtes   ☐ travaux manuels

☐ chansons   ☒ écoute active des histoires
                                  racontées
☒ comptines
                              ☐ exercices de prononciation

Pourquoi? _Dans les histoires ont apprend_
des mots comme "eggs" aussi les
réflexions quand on comprenait pas
on pouvait demandé.

4 Quels bénéfices as-tu retirés de l'apprentissage de l'anglais cette année?

> J'ai appris beaucoup de choses.
> On a appris plus de mots de
> vocabulaire.

5 Aimerais-tu apprendre une autre langue étrangère?

Laquelle? _Espagnole_

Pourquoi? _parce que je conais déjà quelques mots des chiffres._

6 Aimerais-tu continuer à apprendre l'anglais l'année prochaine?

(Oui?) Non?

Pourquoi? _J'aimerais parlé l'anglais très bien._

7 Si oui, souhaiterais-tu que ton professeur d'anglais pratique les mêmes activités que cette année ou préférerais-tu des activités et du matériel nouveaux?

Lesquels? _J'aimerais que se sois des livres nouveax prendre les même pratique que nous appris jusqu'aujourd'hui._

8 Est-ce que tu as d'autres commentaires?

> Je voulais aussi dire que nous avons
> appris plein de chose l'orthographe
> était plus facile que le français.

Thank you!

Figure 5   Self-assessment questionnaire 2 (French)

End of year evaluation

1 Have you enjoyed learning English this year?

(Yes)   No

Why? Why not? _I wanted to learn another language so I wasn't doing just French because I wanted to discover it before we did it in secondary school._

2 Which story did you prefer?

☐ The Snowman   ☐ The Very Hungry Caterpillar
☐ Meg and Mog   ☐ Pat the Cat
☒ Meg's Eggs

Why? _I liked this story very much because I love prehistoric animals._

3 Which activities or exercises did you find the most useful?

☐ picture dictation   ☒ language awareness
☐ number dictation   ☐ tests
☐ classifying   ☐ drama
☐ questions and answers   ☐ drawing
☐ questionnaires and surveys   ☐ handicrafts
☐ songs   ☒ storytelling
☐ rhymes   ☐ pronunciation exercises

Why? _In the stories you learn words like 'eggs'. I also liked the language awareness because when you didn't understand you could ask._

will need to help them establish the criteria they will use to judge their performance. Figures 4 and 5 show two examples of self-assessment questionnaires that were used with pupils in France in the middle of their first year of learning English and at the end of

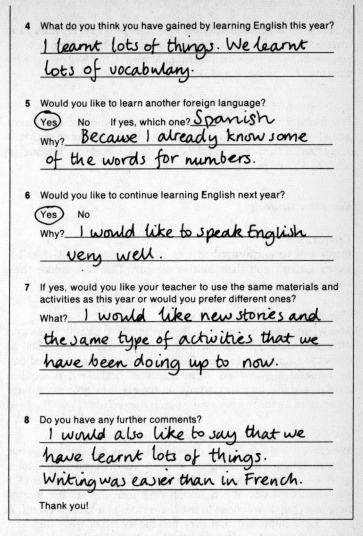

4 What do you think you have gained by learning English this year?

I learnt lots of things. We learnt lots of vocabulary.

5 Would you like to learn another foreign language?

(Yes) No   If yes, which one? *Spanish*

Why? *Because I already know some of the words for numbers.*

6 Would you like to continue learning English next year?

(Yes) No

Why? *I would like to speak English very well.*

7 If yes, would you like your teacher to use the same materials and activities as this year or would you prefer different ones?

What? *I would like new stories and the same type of activities that we have been doing up to now.*

8 Do you have any further comments?

I would also like to say that we have learnt lots of things. Writing was easier than in French.

Thank you!

Figure 5a   Self-assessment questionnaire 2 (English)

the year. Storybooks were used as the principal teaching material. This kind of reflection can help pupils become more aware of themselves and of each other and that individual differences exist, as well as help them evaluate their own progress.

Self-correction

Where possible, choose activities which allow pupils to check their own work either individually or in pairs. This helps them take on responsibility for their own learning and work out where and why they may have made a mistake.

Selecting activities

It is useful from time to time to give pupils a selection of different activities to choose from. This allows pupils to choose activities according to their own interests and needs, decide for themselves what to do, and plan their own work.

Cognitive strategies

Comparing

Pupils can be encouraged to spot differences and similarities be-tween English and their mother tongue. This can arouse their curiosity about language and develop language awareness.

Classifying

Many language learning activities get pupils to classify items into different groups, for example, hot or cold, sweet or salty, wild or domestic animals and so on. This revises a basic concept and can be a useful memory aid when learning vocabulary. It requires pupils to think and sort words or objects into different groups determined by the teacher or the pupils themselves.

Developing an awareness of visual and audio clues

We make use of a variety of clues to help work out meaning in our mother tongue, for example, tone of voice, facial expressions, gestures, visual support, and so on. This is usually done at a subconscious level. When deciphering meaning in the foreign language, pupils will need to use these clues to a greater extent. It is therefore important that they become aware of what they are. Many of the activities described in Chapters 6, 7 and 8 on listening, reading and vocabulary develop this awareness. This conscious knowledge of how visual and audio clues can aid understanding will in turn enhance pupils' performance in their mother tongue.

Predicting

Pupils can be encouraged to anticipate what they think might come next in a spoken or written message. When involving pupils in activities that encourage anticipation, it is important that the teacher accepts all appropriate suggestions even if they do not correspond exactly with what is said or happens. The main aim here is to encourage pupils to anticipate the general meaning, for example, what could happen or what could be said and then to check whether their expectations match the reality of what they actually hear or read. This involves pupils actively and personally in the learning process and can develop self-confidence. Predicting is also useful as a strategy for pupils to use in their mother tongue.

Risk-taking

It is important that pupils build up enough confidence so they are willing to take risks when learning a foreign language. This will equip them for occasions when they do not have a teacher with them, another pupil to ask, or a dictionary to look up a word in, and so on. The teacher can encourage risk-taking by inviting pupils to guess the meaning of words they do not know; attempting to pronounce a new word; hypothesizing; discussing a learning strategy; and so on.

Organizing work

Work related to the English lesson can be organized and stored in different ways: in an exercise book or a folder and labelled and dated; as personal vocabulary sets, made by cutting out pictures, colouring and labelling; as personal picture dictionaries; as rhyme or song books; and so on. Pupils can also collect pictures and make collages of specific language examples, for example, food packets, clothes labels, shop signs, and so on.

Using reference materials

Pupils can learn how to use a dictionary effectively. This may be a picture dictionary, a bilingual dictionary or a dictionary with simple definitions in English. Pupils can also learn to use a book corner efficiently and to look for other books related to a particular subject, for example, dinosaurs, butterflies, monsters, and so on.

Social mediation strategies

Pair or group work

Working with each other in pairs or groups provides pupils with the opportunity for taking on responsibility for their own learning by working independently of the teacher for part of a lesson. It can also involve them in planning and directing their own work.

It is important to remember that many of the strategies described above for learning English can also be applied to other subject areas. The children should be reminded of this when appropriate so that they learn to transfer strategies and develop an overall awareness of their learning across the curriculum.

Part 3   The teacher's role

10   Selecting materials

There is an abundance of English language teaching material available on the market, covering different aspects of language learning and language use. It ranges from general courses, in several volumes and supported by visual and taped materials, to specialized books which concentrate on one aspect of English, such as vocabulary, or one specific skill, such as listening, or books containing collections of games, songs, rhymes, etc. Faced with this vast range of teaching material available, what are some of the key questions the teacher should ask to select appropriate materials for their particular teaching context?

Aims and objectives

It is important to bear in mind the basic aims of learning English at both primary and secondary levels. In other words, you need to relate the teaching materials to your aims and objectives. When teaching a foreign language at primary level, it is important that the teaching is not a watered-down version of aims and methodology used at the secondary level.

Familiarize yourself with the aims of your teaching programme and any Ministry documents that provide guide-lines. The central idea of the French experimentation, for example, with important consequences on the selection (or production) of teaching materials, is the fact that children beginning to learn a foreign language two years earlier – at 9 years old instead of 11 – are not meant to learn what they would previously have learnt between 11 and 13 (see Chapter 5). The basic aim is to prepare children to benefit fully from the language teaching they will get at secondary school. Psychologically, this means that they will become aware that what they say and write in their mother tongue can be said and written in another language in other forms, other sounds and rhythms, other spellings, and that one can sing and play and have fun in another language. Linguistically and culturally, this means they will learn new phenomena and ways of living, through different aspects of everyday life.

It is important that the teaching materials used should take the learner forward as directly as possible towards your aims and objectives. The objectives should be decided first, in line with the overall aims of the teaching programme, and then materials should be sought which can be related to these objectives. The aims of the teaching programme should determine the materials to be used and not vice versa.

Methodology

The general methodology associated with primary teaching, for example, an active participation by the pupils (learning by doing), frequent recycling, a great use of visual aids, objects, models, puppets, songs and games, etc., must contribute to the general aim of all subjects taught at that level and is also an important criterion for the selection of materials. See Chapter 4 for further details.

Learning activities must present and practise English in a systematic and comprehensive way so that new language items can be assimilated by the pupil. There is sometimes a tendency when working with young learners to use activities for their own sake, because they are enjoyable or because they 'work' as activities, without due regard to their value as language learning exercises. The things our pupils do in class should be interesting and enjoyable, but they should also be carefully examined in terms of their language teaching and learning potential and how they relate to what has previously been learnt and what is to be learnt.

Choosing a coursebook

Why use a coursebook?
Most teachers of English use a coursebook and there are a number of good reasons for doing so.

- It is a useful learning aid for the pupil.
- It can identify what should be taught/learnt, and the order in which it should be taught/learnt.
- It can indicate what methodology should be used.
- It can provide, attractively and economically, all or most of the materials needed.

Some teachers may use one coursebook only, taking their pupils through it from beginning to end, whilst others may take materials from several different books, adapting them where necessary and supplementing them with original material they have produced themselves. It is rare, however, to meet a teacher who does not, to a greater or lesser extent, draw on published teaching material, as producing original materials is a difficult and time-consuming process. Many coursebooks, however, are general in that they are designed to satisfy a general world-wide market and are meant to be as usable in Brazil as they would be in France. Such courses do not have one particular group of learners in mind and therefore usually take an English-speaking country as a setting along with corresponding sets of cultural values. The teacher should formulate objectives with the needs of the learners in mind and then seek out published materials which will achieve those objectives. No teacher should allow the coursebook to set the objectives, let alone allow 'teaching the coursebook' to be the objective.

In reality, the coursebook often becomes the teaching programme, and the aims and objectives of the book will be adopted for the course. If the teacher has established that the aims of the course and those of the coursebook are reasonably complementary, there seems limited reason for objection. However, the chosen text must be adapted to the particular requirements of the class.

Teachers who express their teaching objectives in terms such as 'finishing unit 9', 'doing the first five chapters' or 'reaching page 68' are acting as a servant of the coursebook rather than as its master. In other words, the coursebook is a menu from which you choose, rather than a recipe which you follow.

What coursebooks say about themselves

Different courses have different aims and claim to reach different objectives. It is useful to look at what some of the coursebooks say about themselves. As can be seen, there is a variety of aims and methodology that abound in the world of English language teaching materials.

> *Outset* is a three-level primary English course for beginners. It is stimulating and simple for pupils and teachers to use. Language learning is through experience first, explanation and practice second, but above all through the pupils' interest in what comes next.
> (*Outset* 1, Macmillan, 1987)

> *SNAP!* develops the four main language skills in a gradual and parallel way. *SNAP!* presents language in contexts that are of immediate interest to children and teaches the language that children need in order to communicate successfully in English. *SNAP!* sensibly limits the amount taught in each lesson and there is constant in-built revision.
> (*SNAP!*, Heinemann, 1983)

The topics, tasks and activities, games and songs are all designed to make learning enjoyable and to help children use English meaningfully in a variety of contexts.

The syllabus takes into account the child's educational and social development as well as providing thorough coverage and recycling of key vocabulary, functions, structures and skills.

(*Stepping Stones*, Thomas Nelson & Sons Ltd, 1992)

Early Bird 1 is a truly activity based course. It teaches a wide range of valid primary school activities through the medium of English. It is an all round educational experience, not just a language course.

(*Early Bird*, Cambridge University Press, 1989)

Chatterbox makes learning easy with an exciting serial story. It involves children in a variety of fun activities. It follows a carefully graded syllabus which allows for recycling of language.

(*Chatterbox*, OUP, 1989)

A wide variety of communicative exercises and activities form the core of the course, providing children with the opportunity to use language meaningfully. The activities include children's games, puzzles and riddles, instructions for making and using things, rhymes and songs and stories for listening and reading.

(*English Today!* OUP, 1985)

As can be seen, these extracts highlight different approaches to English language teaching, for example, topic-based, activity-based, etc. (See Chapter 12) Coursebooks are in no way bound to adopt one approach to the exclusion of all others and many attempt to achieve a working balance between them.

Which of the above descriptions corresponds most closely with your aims and objectives? Why?

Here is a checklist of questions to ask when selecting primary EFL coursebooks.

General questions

- What sort of approach does the book appear to adopt?

- Does one approach predominate? If yes, what are the implications of this in relation to the rest of the curriculum?

- How are new teaching points graded? How frequently are they introduced and how much practice material separates them?

- Is the organization of the course linear or cyclical? Linear – teaching points are added one at a time, each being practised before moving on to the next. Cyclical – a particular teaching point recurs in a different context to be enlarged on throughout the course. What are the implications of this to young learners?

- Are there any special pages of units for revision, self-testing, or reference?

- What are the art work and layout like? Are they attractive? Are they useful or only decorative?

- Does the course include examples of authentic language and materials?

- Does the course include workbooks, tests, tapes, videos, etc.?

- Is the teacher's book easy to follow? Does it contain an index?

- Does the material have a specific cultural setting or is it non culture-specific? If culture-specific, will this be acceptable to your learners?

- Can you spot any notable omissions? Will you have to supplement the coursebook in any way?

Specific questions

Take a sample unit and ask yourself the following questions:

- How is each unit titled? Will it be clear to your pupils what it is they are expected to learn in the unit?

- How is new language presented?
  - In the form of a continuous story?
  - Through familiar situations (for example, a birthday party)?
  - Through topics?
  - Through activities?

- Does the presentation of new language force the teacher to follow the unit sequence of the coursebook?

- How much new language is presented in each unit? Is the rate at which new material is introduced appropriate for your pupils?

- What kind of practice activities are there? Is there an appropriate balance between controlled and freer practice? Are they motivating and meaningful?

- Is fluency catered for in addition to accuracy?

- How much variety of activity is there?

- How is new vocabulary presented?

- Does the book offer mother tongue translation? Do you regard this as useful or not?

- Is there an opportunity for reviewing at the end of each unit?

- How are the different skills treated? Are they integrated?

Choosing supplementary materials

Although the coursebook may provide the bulk of most teachers' materials, many make use of other materials from time to time in order to provide variety. There are a great number of supplementary materials available for the teaching of English as a foreign language. These include graded and authentic storybooks, dictionaries, nursery rhymes, songs, activity books, cassettes, videos, games, and so on.

When choosing supplementary materials, look at them carefully asking yourself how they relate to:

- the language presented in your coursebook
- the type of supplementary language and practice they will provide
- your pupils' motivation.

For example, some rhymes and songs contain obscure and specialized language forms. Try to select materials that will reinforce and consolidate structures and vocabulary presented in your coursebook.

When selecting supplementary materials, you can also look at authentic materials (materials not written specifically for the teaching of English as a foreign language). For example, many games that children know in their mother tongue can be played in the foreign language. You may like to make a collection of children's comics, toys, posters, and so on, to decorate the classroom. See Chapter 11 for ideas on classroom display.

See also Chapter 13 for a detailed list of criteria to use for selecting storybooks and Chapter 14 for using games, songs and rhymes.

Producing your own materials

As already mentioned, producing your own materials can be a
time-consuming process, so how often you do this will depend on
the amount of time you have available and your particular needs.
Most teachers, however, produce their own worksheets, flashcards,
visual aids, games, and so on, from time to time. Think about
some of the reasons why you may do this.

Here are some suggestions:

1 You may feel that your coursebook does not provide enough
practice and you need to supplement it by adding some extra
exercises.

2 The activities, exercises or visual aids in your coursebook may
not be very interesting or may be inappropriate for your class,
so you may decide to adapt them to make them more suitable or
to make original ones.

3 You may need to create worksheets because you want to organize your class in a special way. For example, you may want to
provide your pupils with a selection of different activities to
choose from so that they can work at their own pace. This will
be easier to organize if pupils are given individual worksheets.
See Chapter 11, Classroom management, for further details on
how to organize 'free choice' lessons.

4 You may not have enough coursebooks for each pupil in your
class so will need to make worksheets and visual aids.

5 You may decide to make your own worksheets or visual aids
simply for variety, to make a change from the coursebook.

Making worksheets

Worksheets can be exercises which are drawn, written or typed on
sheets of paper then photocopied or reproduced on a duplicating
machine so that they can be given out to each pupil in the class.
They can be a great help to the teacher for organizing oral
activities in pairs and small groups, and also for simple reading
and writing tasks. If you do not want your pupils to write on or
colour the worksheets, you must say so in advance! If they are
stuck onto or written directly onto pieces of card and covered in
plastic they will last longer and can be used over and over again
with the same class to recycle language in different contexts or
with different classes. Alternatively, if your pupils can keep the
worksheets, they can personalize them by writing their name and

the date, colouring them, and storing them in their English folders or sticking them in their exercise books. This involves pupils more actively in the learning task and teaches useful study skills.

When designing worksheets, think carefully about how you want your pupils to use them. For example, if they are to enable pupils to work in pairs and practise listening and speaking, or to work individually and practise reading and writing. It is a good idea to try out the worksheet yourself before using it with your class. Ask yourself the following questions.

● Are the aims clear? Do I need to write instructions on the worksheet in English/in the pupils' mother tongue, or can I explain the instructions orally?

● Is there enough room to write ticks (√), crosses (×), names, numbers, words, draw pictures, and so on?

● Can the pupils see what language they are practising?

Write or draw clearly in black ink. Do not try to fit too much on to one sheet of paper. The worksheet will look cramped and over-whelm or demotivate the pupil. Focus on one language learning point at a time so that pupils are clear about what they should do and what they are practising.

It is always possible to involve pupils in making their own worksheets and this can be a useful way of linking work in the English language classroom with other subjects in the curriculum. For example, the worksheet on page 98 was made by pupils in their maths class. This involved listening to instructions for making a grid, measuring, and drawing horizontal and vertical lines. They then drew the food items and labelled them and used the worksheet to interview each other about their likes and dislikes.

Here are some further examples of teacher-produced work-sheets.

1 Information gap (Figure 6) Pupils work in pairs, A and B. The following instructions can be given orally or written on the work-sheet. However, as pupils become familiar with pair work and information gap activities, you will not need to give the same basic instructions every time.

> Work in pairs. Do not show each other your worksheet.
> Pupil B begin. Ask pupil A, 'How many lemons are there?'
> Pupil A reply, 'There are 7 lemons.'
> Pupil B complete your chart.
> Continue.

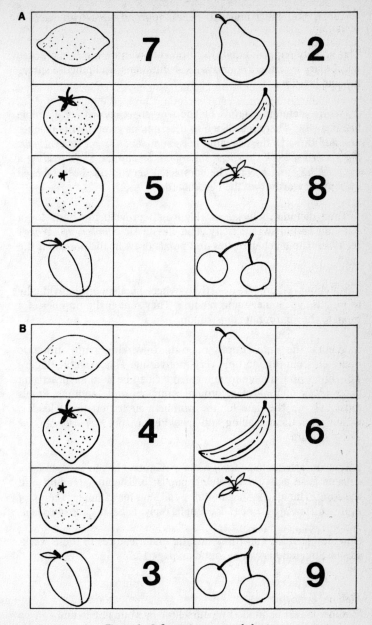

Figure 6 Information gap worksheet

When you have finished, check your answers with each
other.

This activity requires pupils to co-operate with each other, practise
vocabulary for fruit, ask and answer questions, and practise speaking and listening.

2 Picture dictation (Figure 7) The worksheet consists of a simple
line drawing. The pupils listen to descriptions given by the teacher
and add these to the drawing. For example: *She's got straight hair.
She's wearing black stockings, she's got a broomstick, she's wearing a
big black hat*, and so on. The completed version has been labelled
by copying words from the blackboard.

3 Time dictation Clockfaces (Figure 8) provide the basis for a
question and answer activity. The class asks: *Number one. What's
the time?* The teacher replies and pupils draw in the hands on the
clock.

4 Matching (Figure 9) An activity where pupils work individually
to practise vocabulary and reading. They match the number of a
room to the appropriate illustration.

5 What's the date? Pupils often find working with authentic
materials from time to time very motivating. This example (Figure
10) shows how a page from a calendar can be used for practising
dates (days of the week, ordinal numbers and months). Pupils
must tell you the date for the numbers circled on the calendar,
which gives them reading and speaking practice: *It's Monday, the
2nd of January.*

6 True or false? A page from a diary (Figure 11) can be used for a
true or false activity, involving pupils in listening, reading and
speaking. The teacher or another pupil says for example: *The 1st of
April is a Tuesday! True or false?* Pupils reply: *False! It's a Wednesday!*

Now decide what you think are the main features of these worksheets. Suggestions can be found on page 127.

Making flashcards
Flashcards can be made by yourself or by your pupils and can be
used to introduce, practise or review structures and vocabulary.
For young learners, they are very often made by using pictures but

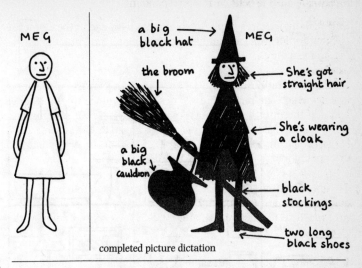

Friday, 17 January 1992

MEG

a big black hat → MEG

the broom

She's got straight hair

She's wearing a cloak

a big black cauldron

black stockings

two long black shoes

completed picture dictation

Figure 7   Picture dictation worksheet

What's the time?
It's _____

1 2 3
4 5 6

Figure 8   Time dictation worksheet

Retrouvez le numéro de chacune des pièces de la maison et inscrivez-le dans le petit carré correspondant.

1 bedroom
2 sitting room
3 bathroom
4 garage
5 kitchen

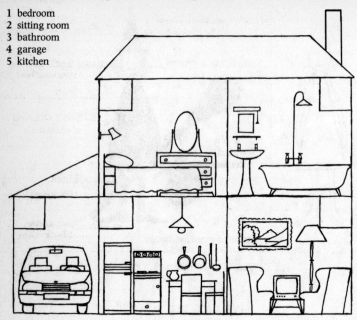

Figure 9   Matching worksheet

JANUARY	FEBRUARY	MARCH
M T W T F S S	M T W T F S S	M T W T F S S
1 ②3 4 5	1 2	①
6 7 8 9 10 11 12	③4 5 6 7 8 9	2 3 4 5 6 7 8
13 14 15 16 17 18 19	10 11 12 13 14 15 16	9 10 11 12 13 14 15
20 21 22 23 24 25 26	17 18 19 20 21 22 23	16 17 18 19 20 21 22
27 28 29 30 31	24 25 26 27 28 29	23 24 25 26 27 28 29
		30 31

APRIL	MAY	JUNE
M T W T F S S	M T W T F S S	M T W T F S S
1 2 3 ④5	1 2 3	1 2 ③4 5 6 7
6 7 8 9 10 11 12	4 5 6 7 8 9 10	8 9 10 11 12 13 14
13 14 15 16 17 18 19	11 ⑫13 14 15 16 17	15 16 17 18 19 20 21
20 21 22 23 24 25 26	18 19 20 21 22 23 24	22 23 24 25 26 27 28
27 28 29 30	25 26 27 28 29 30 31	29 30

Figure 10   What's the date? worksheet

March 1992	1992 April
30 Monday	Thursday **2**
31 Tuesday	Friday **3**
1 Wednesday	Saturday **4**
	Sunday **5**

Figure 11   True or false? worksheet

words can also be used. If the latter, they should be written in large, clear, black letters. Pictures can be drawn by yourself or photocopied. It is useful to enlarge pictures on a photocopier if possible. They can then be coloured by you or your pupils. Pictures can be cut out from magazines. Mail order catalogues are often a useful source for finding pictures. When using flashcards, ask yourself the following questions.

● Are they large enough for the whole class to see?

● Does the picture convey the meaning clearly? For example, for naming an animal, an object, a size – big or small, for describing actions using the present continuous, and so on.

Look at the following set of flashcards. What language points could be practised?

Suggestions can be found on page 127.

A set of flashcards could be used in the following way. The language has already been introduced and now you want to move on to the practice stage.

Show the first card and ask: *Do you come to school by bus, Marc?* Marc replies. Now ask another pupil.

Show the other cards in the same way. You now want the pupils to ask the question. Give a card to a pupil and say, *Valerie, ask Pierre!* Valerie may or may not be able to produce the question. If she can, use her as a model and get the class to repeat. If not, ask another pupil. If necessary, repeat the question yourself and get the class to repeat. Then ask individual pupils again.

When you use flashcards in this way, they act as a prompt because pupils have to find the words themselves. This focuses their attention on meaning and prevents the activity from becoming completely mechanical.

As producing your own materials can be so time-consuming, try to work with other teachers and build up a resource bank. Worksheets and flashcards can be stored and labelled in envelopes, or in folders if they are on single sheets of paper. If they are on card and covered in plastic, they can be stored in boxes. Think carefully about ways you can organize your materials so that they can be found easily.

Worksheet features

● They are clear, simple and attractive.

● The instructions are in very simple English or in the pupils' own language.

● Each worksheet provides an activity which lasts a few minutes.

● There are opportunities for the worksheets to be personalized, for example, coloured, labelled, and so on.

● Each worksheet practises one particular language point, for example, a structure or a lexical set, and involves pupils in different skills and possibilities for linking English with other subjects in the curriculum.

Using flashcards

● Introducing and practising vocabulary related to transport.
Teacher: *What's this?*
Pupil: *It's a bicycle.*

● Introducing and practising *Yes/No* questions or *Wh* questions.
Teacher: *Do you come to school by bicycle?*
Pupil: *Yes, I do. / No, I don't.*

Teacher: *How do you come to school?*
Pupil: *I come to school by bus.* or *By bus.*

● Introducing and practising *can* for expressing ability.
Teacher: *Can you ride a bicycle?*
Pupil: *Yes, I can. / No I can't.*

● Introducing and practising talking about possessions.
Teacher: *Have you got a skateboard?*
Pupil: *Yes, I have. / No, I haven't.*

Can you think of any other language points that could be practised?

References and further reading

Kilroy, S., 1981. *Copycat*: Puffin.
Wright, A., 1984. *A Thousand Pictures for Teachers to copy*: Collins.

Magazines and journals
JET
Modern English Teacher
Practical English Teaching
Standpoints
(See Appendix for subscription details.)

11 Classroom management

In this chapter you will be encouraged to think more carefully about classroom management skills in relation to three specific areas: your own teaching skills, the management of an effective learning environment for your pupils, and ways of organizing the classroom. Classroom management skills include specific routines and actions which teachers use to make their teaching more effective. You might like to ask yourself whether you are good at the following routines and actions, or whether some of these need improvement.

● Organizing learning activities
● Maintaining discipline
● Organizing pair and group work
● Using audio-visual aids, including the blackboard
● Keeping records of work done and children's progress

Teaching skills

Here we will consider some aspects of:

● teachers' language abilities and other talents
● classroom control
● management of time.

Teachers' abilities, talents and skills

Many people argue about the qualities needed to make a good teacher of English to young learners. Is it the primary-trained teacher who may not have a perfect command of English but who has a good understanding of how children think and learn, or is it the teacher who is a fluent and accurate English speaker but who may not be trained in teaching children of primary-school age? The ideal, of course, would be a teacher who combines both these sets of training and skills, but this may in reality form a small minority of teachers who deal with ELT in primary classes.

Many successful teachers may not have a perfect command of English and yet be excellent in engaging children's attention and in creating a purposeful, lively and interesting learning environment. Two of the main factors leading to successful teaching seem to be developing confidence in your language abilities and having a thorough understanding of children and primary education. Two ways in which non-native teachers can develop confidence in their English are:

Preparing in private
Check through the coursebook you might be using or the language activities you have planned and familiarize yourself with the vocabulary and sentence patterns which will be used. This kind of rehearsal is more effective if you do it out loud.

Meeting other English teachers
Teaching can sometimes be a rather isolated profession so it is a good idea to build up an informal network of English teachers in your area. You can then meet occasionally, once a month or once a term, to discuss lessons and share ideas or resources. If you have a teachers' centre or club nearby, it may be useful to suggest a more formal network which might include having a regular language 'clinic' where teachers can check aspects of language use with other colleagues. This is especially useful if some native speakers of English are available for you to ask questions about grammar, pronunciation, or current vocabulary or phrases. You can find out more about assessing your English and improving your use of English in the classroom in Chapters 15 and 16.

When teaching children it is especially beneficial to have certain talents which help to provide variety, to make lessons more enjoyable, or to make English teaching 'come alive'. Perhaps you are good at some of the following things:

● Telling stories
  The ability to tell a story well is very important in the primary classroom. You may do this by using different voices, alternating between soft and loud speech, or using pauses to build up suspense. You can read more about storytelling in Chapter 13.

● Singing or playing an instrument
  These are excellent talents for making songs and rhymes an integral and enjoyable part of your lessons. You can find out more about songs and rhymes in Chapter 14.

● Drawing
  Drawings are very effective in conveying the meaning of a new word or when presenting new language. Even if you are not a natural artist, your drawing techniques can be improved with practice. There are several useful books which provide guidance and ideas for the teacher, such as *Copycat* or *A Thousand Pictures for Teachers to Copy*. Other tips are:
  – Try out your drawing before going into the class.

- Use an overhead projector or flip-chart which allows you to copy and make a set of drawings beforehand.
- Draw a faint outline on the blackboard before the lesson (only possible if you have access to the classroom beforehand).
- Keep the drawing simple and large enough for everyone to see.

● Acting
Being willing to roleplay yourself is especially encouraging if you want the children to do a roleplay activity. You will probably need to demonstrate some of the characters if, for instance, you want them to roleplay going shopping in the Shop Corner, or to act out a story. You may find that with a little encouragement the children are far better than you!

Classroom control and discipline

An area of classroom management which has an important effect on the classroom atmosphere and the amount of learning which takes place concerns discipline and classroom control. The most effective environment for learning is found in a classroom where the teacher is firm but kind and encouraging. Children generally like to work within a framework where the boundaries of acceptable and unacceptable behaviour are reasonable and consistent so that they know where they stand. Children become aware very quickly of teachers who are inconsistent in their standards of discipline or who maintain discipline simply through sarcasm, ridicule or bullying. This can frequently lead to a classroom of passive children who are beaten into quiet submission; in a language learning classroom where we want children to use English freely and actively, this is very undesirable! On the other hand, a classroom with little discipline may descend into chaos, where nothing is learned.

Teaching style is very much a personal matter which develops with experience. Teachers' differing teaching styles lead to different attitudes towards discipline and classroom control. Common variations include the amount of noise or the degree of pupil autonomy which is considered acceptable: in some classrooms pupils may walk around freely, or give answers without always putting up their hand first. You may need to think carefully about exactly what you consider to be unacceptable behaviour in pupils and the steps you might take with pupils when the boundaries you have set are crossed.

Establishing good relationships with children in the class is vital for effective learning. The teacher should set a good example by praising good behaviour, commenting on good work, making helpful suggestions or waiting for quiet before beginning the lesson or a new activity. In other words, the teacher should avoid giving pupils her full attention only when they are misbehaving. This does not mean that bad behaviour should be ignored but that it should be dealt with quickly and without constant scolding. It is also important that teachers should not make idle threats which they cannot or would not carry out. A clear indication needs to be given early on of your classroom rules and your determination to uphold them calmly and fairly. The number of rules you make should be kept to the minimum and the reason for having them should always be explained to the children. They will probably focus on the encouragement of reasonable behaviour and sociability. Older children could be involved in making up a set of classroom rules themselves which they, and you, have to observe!

Praise and encouragement are important in setting the right atmosphere and provide a good model for the children; tale-telling, unfriendly comments and bullying should all be discouraged. It may also be worth considering how competitive an atmosphere you wish to encourage. A sense of failure engenders negative feelings and low self-esteem; those children who are rarely 'winners' may give up trying, evade work, or become disruptive. Try to find something that each child is good at; s/he might be good at drawing, handwriting, providing good ideas for stories, roleplay or helping others.

When the teacher first enters a classroom, it is probably realistic to allow children to talk quietly until you announce that you are ready to begin the lesson. If the children have to come in from another classroom, some teachers like the children to line up outside so that they can establish a calm atmosphere before the children go in. When you want to gain the attention of the whole class try these steps:

● Make an attention-gaining noise such as saying *Right!* or clapping your hands: most but not all children will respond.

● Give a short verbal instruction, such as *Put down your pens and listen*. A few children will continue to talk.

● Quietly name the children still talking: *Jules, stop talking please*. As soon as the children become quiet, start your lesson to keep their attention.

When children are used to you, simply stand in silence and wait for them to become quiet. If they respect you, they will notice your action and become quiet in a few moments. If they do not, you have more work to do. Once the lesson has started and the children are working on tasks that you have set, you may find the children becoming noisy; sometimes this is caused by inappropriacy of the tasks you have chosen. Check through this list to see if the cause of the children's inattention and indiscipline results from your organization of the learning activities:

● Was the task too difficult? Did you explain the task carefully enough or give the class sufficient practice or models to follow? Would more visual support or frameworks in the form of charts or tables make the task more manageable?

● Was the task rather boring and mechanical with too little attempt at contextualization? Some practice is bound to be repetitive but if the children know it is leading to more purposeful language use, it may become more motivating.

● Was the task too easy? The children may also have done similar work before and finish the task more quickly than expected.

● Was there too much 'dead time' for the able and slow learners? If there is not a sufficient range of tasks at different levels, the able learners will always finish more quickly, while the slower learners may cope with the task by finishing it quickly but in a very superficial manner. You may occasionally need to organize variations of a main language task at different levels so that it is not only the 'average' child who is catered for.

When language activities are pitched at the wrong level or are too mechanical, the children will become frustrated and noisy. You will need to move around the class checking on the children's needs and abilities so that you can modify the task accordingly. When preparing and planning work, try to think of extension activities for the more able, and more structured steps to help slower learners.

If the children are engaged in communicative activities to develop fluency in pairs or groups, the noise level will naturally rise. Most language teachers would find this acceptable, as long as the talk is 'on-task'. If the noise level rises too much, pick out the noisiest group, name one of the children in the group and gesture them to quieten down. The teacher needs to tune in to the class constantly to keep the noise at an acceptable level. Remember that the noisier the teacher is, the noisier the children will become.

When children misbehave during explanations or storytelling with the whole class, try pausing and making eye contact with the child; this avoids interrupting the activity too much. If the child continues, try quietly saying his/her name; with older children ask a direct question. Thus, instead of constantly reprimanding children, ask a question to gain their attention and to keep that of the other children. If the child cannot answer, ask another child and praise him/her for doing so.

Children are often asked to put their hands up before speaking. This is a convenient way of preventing lots of noisy interruptions, although, if applied too rigidly, it may dampen children's natural enthusiasm and spontaneity. It may be most useful when the children are working individually and require help or when they are working in groups. You could try thinking about when you want the children to raise their hands before speaking and explain to the class what you expect. To encourage every child to have a turn and to keep the attention of the whole class, it is useful to ask a question or ask for ideas or suggestions and only then name a specific child or group to respond. The teacher will have to decide how much English will be used to maintain order; the amount will probably increase with the children's age and language level.

Children of primary school age easily become restless, so a rigid restriction of their movement is generally unrealistic. When carrying out group activities, the children should be able to move around freely when necessary to find equipment, make a survey, and so on. If you are not happy with this kind of atmosphere, it is worth ensuring that you sometimes punctuate lessons with more activities, such as games or action songs and rhymes.

Time management
Inexperienced teachers frequently have problems with pacing their lessons. Even more experienced teachers can be over-optimistic about how much can be done in a lesson or despair that they will ever have enough time to work through a scheme of work or syllabus. It is very useful to train yourself to plot realistic timings for the completion of certain activities; this avoids having to rush, which may lead to inattention or ineffective learning. On the other hand, you may be left with time to spare at the end of the lesson, in which case you need to have some activities 'up your sleeve'. These generally include songs or rhymes, games or puzzles; it is worth knowing several well enough so that you can select one which fits in with the current teaching points, or revises a point recently covered.

When ending a lesson, here are several points to bear in mind:

● Try not to finish in the middle of an activity.

● Finish work on the main teaching point a little early rather than late; you can always find a short song, rhyme or game to fill up a few minutes.

● If you want to give out homework, take time to explain it beforehand and give an example. Avoid squeezing it in at the very end of the lesson.

● Try to give praise and encouragement about what the children have achieved during the class.

Establishing routines for setting up groups or using equipment is also vital if you wish to avoid wasting time. Ways of doing this will be discussed in the third part of this chapter.

The pupils' learning environment

In this section we will look at ways of finding out about your pupils and of keeping track of the work they do in the English class.

Finding out about your pupils

It is important that the teacher of English gets to know her pupils; this involves finding out their names, their backgrounds and interests, their previous language learning experience and their attitudes to English. If you are a general classroom teacher, then doing this is less difficult as you will probably be with the same class for most of the day. If however, you are a specialist working with different classes two or three times a week, this is more of a problem.

LEARNING YOUR PUPILS' NAMES

The first step in getting to know your pupils is learning their names. This is important as it helps to identify who should respond in the class and aids the organization of pair and group work. It is invaluable in matters of classroom control as you can identify troublemakers more easily and it helps to show that you care about your pupils. Finally, it leads to the establishment of a friendly and secure atmosphere. You will have to decide whether you are going to address the pupils by their original names or whether you want to give them special English names. It would probably be a good idea to ask the children to vote for their preference. A useful list of English first names and surnames can be found in the book on language games written by Lee (1965).

Many primary classes have fewer than thirty-five children; learning names for larger classes can become quite problematical. A five-point action plan could be:

- Copy out class lists and the names of children you commonly put into groups; write their name on any pieces of work you collect or display to familiarize yourself with the names.

- If you call a register, look at the children as they respond.

- Ask the children to write their names clearly on a piece of card which they place on their desks. If you collect them in and distribute them at the beginning of each lesson you will gradually learn the names well.

- Keep a seating plan of the class. At first you may wish the children to remain in the same seats, although it would be a pity to let this organizational convenience dominate your decision to let the children work in different groups once you know their names.

- If you have given the pupils English names, playing a game will help them (and you) to remember these. Organize the class into groups of 6–8 and ask each child in turn to go round the group (starting with the person on their right) and name each child. Follow this by giving each group a ball or orange; one child begins by naming another child as they throw it to him or her to catch and so on. If you sit in on a few groups as they play, you will have to learn the names quickly!

FINDING OUT ABOUT PUPILS' BACKGROUNDS AND INTERESTS

Again, if you are the general class teacher as well as English teacher, this is something you will have plenty of time to do. If you are not, it is worth spending a little time with the class teacher to find out more about the class. Most primary schools keep records with details of the children's home background and any health problems there may be. If a child has hearing problems, or difficult home circumstances, this may have to be taken into account in seating arrangements or in setting homework. All this should, of course, be done discreetly and without making a fuss or stereotyped generalizations about children's capabilities.

Find out from the children or their class teacher what sorts of topics they have studied already and which were particularly well received. Ask the children what their hobbies are, which clubs they are in, what their favourite games, toys, sports, TV programmes, music, films or people are. This will help you to build up a picture of popular school-based and personal topics which you can draw upon in your lessons to make them interesting and fun. You can do this by talking to the children and filling in a chart as an aide-memoire, or by asking the children to carry out surveys and record the information they discover. With young beginners, this may have to be done first of all in their mother tongue, but with older children this is good English practice.

PUPILS' PREVIOUS LANGUAGE LEARNING EXPERIENCE AND ATTITUDES TO ENGLISH

In the primary school, some children may already speak two languages at home and will thus tend to have a greater awareness of and facility for language learning. Some children may have an English-speaking parent, may have lived in an English-speaking country or may holiday in such countries. Some children may also be having extra English lessons outside school hours. This means you may have to make allowances for children who have a more sophisticated level of English than the rest of the class and who may become bored or disruptive. This can often be avoided by acknowledging these children's previous learning as a bonus (some teachers unfortunately attempt to ignore it), by encouraging the children to share some of their experiences, to help others in groups (but without allowing the group to be dominated), and by sometimes including individualized work at a higher level. It also means making higher demands on these children and not allowing their work to become slip-shod.

Many children today, especially those living in urban areas or those with access to English-speaking programmes on the television, will have a fairly positive attitude to English. This is usually reinforced by the enthusiasm and interest of the teacher which some teachers develop by trips to English-speaking countries. Children will love to hear about your visits and older ones will be fascinated by tape-recordings of English children singing songs, rhymes or telling simple jokes. Advertising in many countries now includes English words and phrases while pop music and cartoons often use English. You might like to make a survey of the use of English in the children's community and ask them to bring in examples of anything they can find using English. This might include food packets, clothing labels, advertisements, newspapers and cartoons, signs and notices. Alternatively, you could ask them to list all the English words they see on slogans, car stickers, and so on. This kind of 'language awareness' is an important part of children's language learning and development.

Record-keeping

An important part of a teacher's duties is keeping track of her pupils' progress. This may be a formal or informal process: if the former, the school will probably have official forms to complete for

each child. These may consist of checklists of items or skills which
the teacher ticks. These can be used to detail grammatical points,
such as tenses; word families, such as clothes; or language skills,
such as listening. If informal records are kept then you can keep a
notebook with comments on each child. If your school uses tests
then you will probably keep a record of the children's marks. The
problem with tests is that they examine children's knowledge of
easy-to-test items, such as vocabulary, grammar or spelling and
leave out other facets of children's learning, such as willingness to
contribute in class, attitude to language learning, skills in writing
stories or taking part in roleplay.

Another form of record the teacher needs to keep is one which
serves as an aide-memoire of language points taught or stories and
topics used in a term. This information can be written down in a
notebook for each class. Information about work covered during a
series of lessons can also be made public for the class to see and to
use. Large charts placed on the wall show which children have
completed particular activities. This is especially useful if you use
pair or group work. For example, if the class has worked on the
story *The Turnip* (in *The Fairy Tale Treasury*) for a few lessons, there
may be a 'free choice' lesson with five different activities the
children can choose from. To keep track of which activities have
been chosen, the children can sign their names alongside (see
Figure 12).

Charts such as these are also useful for keeping track of homework activities (if you set any). Older children may also be encouraged to keep their personal record of work they have done which
summarizes the language and learning skills they have covered.

Organizing the classroom

This final section looks at activities and routines centred on the
classroom itself, such as classroom organization and layout, organizing pair and group work, display and the use of audio-visual aids.

Classroom organization and layout
Careful planning of your classroom is very important as it helps
to create an organized and secure atmosphere. In an ideal situation, you would be able to organize the classroom in the way
you think is most effective for children's learning. In practice, you
may not have total freedom to re-organize the layout of the
classroom in the way that you would wish. However, if you have
some possibilities of doing this, here are six points for you to
consider:

Activity	Names
1 Listen and sequence (Listen to the story on cassette and sequence pictures.)	Louise Phillipe
2 Read and match (Read speech bubbles and match these to different characters.)	Carlos Anna Maria
3 Classifying (Sort shells of different sizes and label these *small, bigger, biggest*.)	Frederico
4 Design seed packets (Draw and write the wording for a seed packet.)	
5 Vegetable printing (Use vegetables to design a cover for a class book on *The Turnip*.)	

Figure 12   Storybook activity record card

1 A grid plan made to scale is especially useful if you have a large class squeezed into a small area. Round tables take up more space than square or rhomboid tables. If your school has a special 'language classroom' where all classes come to learn English, you will have ample opportunities to plan the layout.

2 Think carefully about whether you want the children to sit in rows or groups. Primary schools often have tables arranged in groups to seat 4–6 children, which makes pair and group work easier.

3 If you decide to have a 'teaching base', make sure you have a clear view of the whole room. Although you may have a base in one place, you could try varying your actual teaching position. Research shows that there are 'action zones' where children who sit closest to the teacher concentrate more and work

harder; you need therefore to vary the action zones themselves by changing position or, alternatively, by changing at periodic intervals the children who sit close to you. Don't put trouble-makers at the back of the classroom!

4 A story corner for younger children is also a good idea. This could be carpeted so that they can listen to a story while gathered around you on the floor. A book corner where children can select stories or simple information books to read (such as MacDonald Starters) is also useful. The books could be colour-coded according to difficulty so that the children can select books for themselves or with your guidance. See Chapter 13 for more details on how to set up a book corner.

5 You may also like to include a listening corner which is screened off by cupboards or screens to provide a quiet corner for listening to cassettes of stories or pre-recorded listening activities. With older, more reliable children, a quiet listening corner can some-times be set up temporarily in a corridor or cloakroom outside if there is no space in the classroom. If you do this, the children must know how to operate the cassette on their own and must have clear instructions on the task they are to perform. This task should have a definite outcome, such as a drawing or pictures to sequence and should have been demonstrated and practised beforehand. Make it clear that you will tolerate no misbehaviour as it leads to automatic withdrawal of their right to work unsupervised.

6 Make sure you include some areas to display children's work, using noticeboards, screens or a table.

The layout of the classroom can be varied and sections remodelled by the use of corrugated cardboard to make moveable walls and partitions. It can also be used for display purposes.

Organizing pairs and groups

It is easiest to organize pairs by asking children to work with the child sitting next to them. Occasionally, you might vary this by asking them to work with the child behind. Another idea, when using an information-gap activity, is to have 'tango pairs'. In this set-up, the children sit next to each other away from the table, the first child sitting facing one way, the second child facing in the opposite direction. The children talk over their shoulder to each other, using different sets of information they have in their hands, or working from information you have pinned on opposite walls. This information could take the form of pictures, tables or graphs which one child asks questions about and the other answers, for example, in a guessing game using pictures. Alternatively, there could be different sets of pictures or captions which the children have to match or classify by sharing information.

There are two main ways of organizing groups to work together: one based on the children's choice; the second according to criteria you have established. The first type of group, friendship-based, is the easiest and most popular. These groups often work well together, although you will have to keep an eye on groups composed entirely of troublemakers! It is important that groups do not always remain the same as there may not be a good mix of gender or ability and the children may become bored with working with the same people all the time.

The criteria you select may aim to mix or match the ability level in a pair or group: a bright child may be chosen to help a slower partner; several faster learners may be given a task to stretch them; a group of slower learners may work together at their own pace without feeling rushed by others, and so on. Similarly, it may be undesirable to always have single sex groups. Boys may often refuse to sit with girls and vice versa but generally this should be discouraged.

Classroom display

Children should be encouraged to display their work. Displays make the classroom brighter and more colourful, encourage a purposeful working atmosphere and usually lead to higher motivation and standards since the children's work is made public.

Classroom screens can be constructed cheaply from corrugated cardboard or garden trellises onto which work can be easily pinned. When setting up a display keep the following points in mind:

- Try to keep the work at children's eye level: you want to encourage them to look at it.

- Displays should encourage reading and listening as well as looking: there may be written questions for children to answer or a tape children have made to listen to.

- Titles and lettering should be large and attractive.

- Always try to double-mount pictures, i.e. stick them onto a coloured background or mount.

- Link or co-ordinate work through colours.

- Use boxes covered in brightly coloured cloth to create differences in height for models etc.

- If resources are scarce, ask local firms if they have any brightly coloured off-cuts of card, or unwanted computer paper or wall-paper.

- Use old wallpaper as cheap backing material for written work or pictures.

- Write the child's name on all work.

- Ensure that all children have something on display, not just the bright children.

It is a good idea to link art work with written work. For example, if the writing is about balloons, display the work on cut-out shapes of a balloon. If the children write a story about the old woman who lived in a shoe, make the book into the shape of a shoe. Other ideas using shapes for display of work might include transport, witches, monsters, houses, leaves, animals, and so on.

To save space, children's written work can be displayed on a zig-zag folding book made by folding a length of card into a zig-zag shape. Children's work can then be pasted onto each section. If you cut slits in the front or back sections and thread through a strip of card it helps to make the shape stronger and more stable.

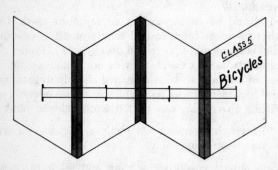

Quick and effective lettering is crucial to your display; felt tip pens are useful for lettering and outlining. Be creative about the shape of the letters you use as titles. You may be able to reflect the themes of the work by using different shaped letters and pictures. For example, you could use old coins to form the title COINS for work on English money, or use letters cut out from newspapers for a simple class newspaper.

Using audio-visual aids
If you are a specialist English teacher travelling from room to

room, you may like to organize a portable teachers' resource box. Find a large box and include things you might find useful in lessons:

- everyday objects, such as a toothbrush, comb, mirror, to demonstrate actions using the present continuous tense

- puppets or masks, to act out dialogues or stories

- pictures of animals or larger models of farm or zoo animals, for identifying and describing animals

- large plans of the inside of a house or zoo, to practise prepositional phrases.

The possibilities are endless.

Important pieces of equipment which you are likely to find in the primary language classroom are: a blackboard, a magnetboard or flannelgraph, an overhead projector (OHP), and a cassette player.

Consider how well you use the blackboard by asking yourself the following questions. Do you:

- write clearly and legibly so that children at the back of the class can see?

- organize your blackboard layout so that you avoid writing random words and phrases all over the board?

- avoid speaking for any length of time with your back turned to the class while you write on the blackboard?

- use colours to organize new vocabulary into easily recognizable word families?

- allow opportunities for the children to write on the blackboard?

- use the blackboard as a backdrop for pictures which you can move around for sequencing and classifying activities?

If you answer 'No' to more than two questions, your blackboard skills could do with brushing up!

A magnetboard is a piece of metal painted white on which you can attach pictures or written captions which have magnetic tape stuck to their backs. If you can buy the tape in a stationer's you could try to make your own board if your school does not have one; try not to make it too small. A flannelgraph or feltboard works on the same principle and consists of a piece of material (an old flannelette sheet will do) with special tape attached to the back. They tend to be less effective than the magnetboard however. Try using a magnetboard for:

● attaching pictures to build up a scene when telling a story.

● sequencing a series of pictures or written statements.

● matching pictures to written labels or speech bubbles to characters.

● classifying pictures or words into different families, for example, different kinds of food bought in packets, food bought in tins, or types of clothing for hot weather, wet weather, etc.

An overhead projector is especially useful for producing written work while still facing the class, or for showing prepared work such as charts or graphs, which thus saves time. Why not try using it in these ways:

● Show the class a family tree which you fill in to give them an example.

● Fill in a substitution table used to describe what things are used for, for example:

a toothbrush a comb a watch	is used for	brushing teeth combing hair telling the time

● Complete a tickchart which describes animals and can be used to ask riddles such as *I'm thinking of an animal with no legs. What is it?* For example:

	no legs	2 legs	4 legs
lion	✗	✗	✓
snake	✓	✗	✗
elephant	✗	✗	✓
hen	✗	✓	✗

● Make a class story, using suggestions given by the children.

● Provide an opportunity for children to write or draw things at their desk and then use the OHP to show and talk about their work.

A cassette recorder is useful for presenting dialogues and songs in the class. If you have a listening corner in the classroom, it provides an opportunity for children to listen to a story again at their own pace or to develop their listening skills by 'listen and do' activities. Some of these were described in Chapter 6. You will need to demonstrate the controls to the children, although most of them will be quite familiar with their operation. You will also need to build in a sound signal so that the children can stop and start the tape to complete the activities you request. Another suggestion is to allow the children to tape-record themselves. This is highly motivating although it will take some preparation; it is an excellent vehicle for raising the standards of both fluency and accuracy. Working in pairs or groups, the children could record themselves for the following purposes:

● recording a story for another class (a story they have been told, or one they have made up themselves);

● making up riddles for other children to guess the answer to;

● asking a group of children questions so that they can complete a tickchart to accompany a survey;

● taping a newsletter to send to another school.

You and the children should have fun experimenting with some of these ideas. When you make resources, such as sets of pictures, games or recordings, remember that the children may be able to help you with drawing, sticking, lettering, and so on. This will help to cut down on your preparation time. Also, make sure that you store the materials efficiently in large labelled envelopes, boxes, and so on. It is important to keep a list of these, perhaps with some notes on how to use them so that other teachers can borrow them. It is also useful to number and colour-code them according to topics and/or level of difficulty so that both teachers and the children can find things easily without wasting too much time.

This chapter has tried to illustrate some of the ways teachers can reflect on and perhaps improve their classroom management skills. It is hoped that developing confidence in these skills will make teachers more effective and less stressed. The suggestions aim to create a well-organized, friendly, and interesting learning environment for both teachers and pupils.

References and further reading

Barrs, M. et al, 1988. *The Primary Language Record:* CLPE.

Briggs, R. and V. Haviland, 1974. *The Fairy Tale Treasury:* Puffin.

Halliwell, S., 1991. *Yes – but will they behave? Pathfinder 4:* CILT.

Lee, W., first edition 1965. *Language Teaching games and contests:* Oxford University Press.

Montgomery, D. and A. Rawlings, 1986. *Bright Ideas: Classroom Management:* Scholastic Publications.

Thorogood, J., 1990. *Recording progress, Pathfinder 1:* CILT.

Underwood, M., 1987. *Effective Class Management:* Longman.

Whiteford R. and J. Fitzsimmons, 1988. *Bright Ideas: Display:* Scholastic Publications.

12   Lesson planning

This chapter looks at how individual techniques and activities fit into a lesson as a whole. As Wilga Rivers writes, 'A lesson is not a haphazard collection of more or less interesting items, but a progression of interrelated activities which reinforce and consolidate each other in establishing the learning towards which the teacher is directing his efforts.'

If you are using a coursebook, the teacher's book may contain detailed notes concerning the aims of each lesson, what aspects of language are recycled and points to be taught, the different stages of the lesson and suggestions on how to teach the lesson. If this is your case, you still need, however, to decide how best to teach the lesson. You may prefer alternative ways of approaching a lesson than those suggested by your coursebook. Above all, a coursebook should be used as a menu from which you choose, rather than a recipe which you follow rigidly. Be ready to depart from your coursebook when the needs of your pupils (or syllabus) do not correspond with what is offered by the coursebook. Some teacher's books are inadequate or you may not have one at all; or you may not be using a coursebook, preferring to collect your own materials from a variety of different sources. Whatever your situation, you will need to plan your lessons according to your particular teaching context.

Before the lesson

Before each lesson, it is important to know what the general aims are, how you are expected to achieve them and how each lesson connects with other lessons, past and future. Coursebooks express their aims in different ways depending on how the book is organized. This may be:

- topic-based
  New language is introduced through topics related to the day-to-day reality of children. See Figure 13. The aims of the lesson may be to learn the names of different animals and to practise asking for information.

- Activity-based
  New language is introduced through different activities, such as games, making things, drawing, etc. See Figure 14. The aim of the lesson may be to practise giving simple instructions.

STEPPING STONES

Contents

Introduction to English   page 2

Units 1-5 — Pets

Units 6-10 — The Classroom

Units 11-14 — Family and Friends

Units 15-19 — Toys and Games

Units 20-24 — The Body

Units 25-28 — Clothes

Round-Up Unit   page 60

Figure 13   *Stepping Stones* Course Book 1 by Julie Ashworth and John Clark

- functionally-based
  The aim of the lesson may be to practise describing objects or people. See Figure 15.

- structurally-based
  The aim of the lesson may be to practise *going to*.

- skills-based
  The aim of the lesson may be to practise listening to instructions or to practise talking about your family.

Page	Activities	New language items
1	On the phone	*Hello!*
2–3	Look and do	*I'm ____.*
4–5	Look and do	*Come in. This is ____.*
6–7	A game: *Say 'please'*	*Good morning/afternoon. Stand up/Sit down/Stop/please*
8–9	A game: *Draw and say*	*Yes/No;* vocabulary
10–11	A guessing game	Vocabulary
12–13	Puzzle pictures	Vocabulary
14–15	At the toy shop	*This is ____;* vocabulary
16–17	Making toothpick pictures	*What's this? It's a ____;* vocabulary
18–19	A drawing game	Vocabulary
20–21	A guessing game	*Is it a ____? No, it's a ____;* vocabulary
22–23	Another guessing game	*Is it the ____?*
24–25	Making a mask	*This is my ____;* vocabulary
26–27	Playing with masks	*Yes. I am ____; You are ____.*
28–29	A song	*Happy birthday to you!*
30–31	Rob the robot: See him walk!	*He is a ____; He can; Walk/Stop; Right/Left; Push.*
32–33	A game: *Sam the robot!*	*Point to ____;* vocabulary: the body
34–35	Making Pam the puppet	*She is ____; You can; her; draw/cut/stick/paint*
36–37	A number rhyme to learn	*Numbers 1–10;* vocabulary
38–39	A numbers game: *Go to school*	*Start/finish/go back/go on*
40–41	A counting puzzle	*How many ____?* names of shapes
42–43	Drawing using simple shapes	*It is not a ____;* vocabulary
44–45	Drawing people using simple shapes	*Is he/she a ____?*
46–47	Making peanut puppets	*What is his/her name? His/her name is ____. How are you? Fine, thanks*
48–49	A rhyme to learn	Telling the time; one to twelve o'clock
50–51	A game: *What's the time, Mr. Wolf?*	*Half past/a quarter past/a quarter to*
52–53	A game: *Follow the colours*	Names of colours
54–55	A colour puzzle; making a coloured toy	Vocabulary revision
56–57	Rhymes to learn and say	*I have; he/she has;* vocabulary revision
58–59	A little story to act	*Is this your ____? I don't know. Thank you.*
60–61	A game: *Lost property*	*My ____ is small/big/short/long/clean/dirty*
62–63	Seven riddles to answer	More practice with adjectives
64	A conversation	General revision

Figure 14   *English Today!* Pupil's Book 1 by D. H. Howe

● situationally- or story-based
   Many coursebooks introduce new language in situations or contexts that are familiar to children and units are given titles such as, 'How old are you?' (Figure 16) or 'Our House' (Figure 17).

Most coursebooks combine more than one of the above aims but the way a lesson is organized will help you see its particular focus. When clarifying the aims of a lesson, it is important not only for you to think about what language and skills you are going to teach but also what your pupils will learn to do in the lesson.

Language summary

	Functional areas	Expressions*	Vocabulary*
Steps 1–15	Identification Quantity	Look/Look at I am, it is What is this? Is it a . . . ? Yes/No How many?	Small letters *a–s* Numbers *1–6* Nouns beginning with *a–s*
Steps 16–30	Description	What colour is . . . ? What is this word/ letter/number? Point to . . .	Small letters *t–z* Nouns beginning with *t–z* Classroom objects Colours *big/little*
Steps 31–45	Possession	I have, Sue has How old are you?	Toys *my*
Steps 46–60	Revision of Steps 1–45	Revision of Steps 1–45	Numbers *7–10* Parts of the body Shapes

*At the back of this book there is a complete list of the words used in the text of the Pupil's Book.
The Teacher's Book gives full guidance on the language syllabus and its presentation to the pupils.

Figure 15   *Get Ready!* **Pupil's Book 1, OUP, 1988**

Writing a lesson plan

The writing of a lesson plan can help you define and clarify your aims as well as prepare the lesson, as it helps you decide what to do and how you will do it. It also provides you with a written record of what you have done which you can look at again after the lesson to evaluate what happened (see Figure 18). You could also use the plan again with another class.

There is no 'correct' way to write a lesson plan, but it should give a clear picture of what you intend to do. To start off, you may find it helpful to use a lesson planning sheet like the one in Figure 18 on page 153.

First, define your aims. The way you order these may vary according to the focus of your language materials: whether they are topic-based, structurally-based, etc. Notice that a category has been included on the sheet for learning to learn activities. Such activities aim to focus the pupil's attention on the process of learning; in other words, on how they learn in addition to what they learn (See Chapter 9, on learning to learn, for further details.) Figure 18 shows an example of a lesson plan focusing on

Figure 16 *Chatterbox*, Pupil's Book 1 by Derek Strange and J. A. Holderness

how to describe a person. Once you have defined your aims, you need to decide how you are going to achieve them. A lesson needs shape: a beginning, a middle and an end.

Figure 17   *Treasure Trail*, Book 1 by Margaret Iggulden and Julie Allen

Procedures

A possible set of procedures might be:

Warm-up   This could take the form of an informal chat aimed at building up and maintaining rapport with your pupils. It could also include the ritual activities of taking the register, writing the date on the blackboard, talking about the weather, etc.

Revision of relevant language   This is to consolidate an earlier lesson

Lesson planning sheet

Date _10 January 1992_

Class _9-10 year-olds, first year of English_

Length of lesson _45 minutes_

Materials _Meg & Mog + cassette (Puffin Books 1972)_
The Storytelling Handbook (Penguin English 1991)

Aims	
Structural	She's got . . . She's wearing . . .
Functional	Describing a person
Skills	Listening for specific information Speaking
Phonological	'h' as in 'hat' /əʊ/ as in 'cloak'
Lexical	clothes: hat, shoes, cloak, stockings adjectives: tall, big, long, straight, curly revision of colours
Learning to learn	Reviewing pre- and post-lesson Awareness of visual clues as aids to meaning, eg mime, drawing Working independently of teacher: pairwork
Assumptions:	Pupils already know some vocabulary for clothes and colours.

Figure 18

Procedures

Time		Activity	Aids
of lesson	of each stage		
1.30	5	<u>Warm up and review</u> of work covered last lesson: names of main characters & animals.	
1.50	15	<u>Presentation</u>: Show pupils cover of book & point to Meg. Ask, 'What's she wearing?' Elicit vocabulary for clothes. Encourage pupils to say, 'She's wearing a hat' etc. Introduce adjectives. Convey meaning through mime & drawing.	Cover of book
2.00	10	<u>Practice</u>: Picture dictation. Distribute pictures of Meg. Explain instructions. Dictate instructions, eg 'She's wearing a tall, black hat'. Pupils draw (see p.123)	Work-sheet
2.10	10	<u>Production</u>: Revise other vocabulary for clothes & colours & structure, 'She's wearing'. Explain activity to pupils. Pairwork: Pupil A describes a pupil to the class without saying his/her name. Pupil B guesses who it is. Change over.	
2.15	5	<u>Review</u>: What have we done today? What have you learnt today? Which activity did you prefer? Why? Did the activities help you learn? How?	

and provide a base for input of new language. It can be very useful: it encourages pupils to reflect on what they learnt and did in the previous lesson. It can also provide you with valuable information about what your pupils learnt and what was significant to them in the lesson.

Explanation of what is to be learnt and done in the lesson Pupils also need to know the aim of the lesson as a whole and the purpose of each procedure. It is important that each part of the lesson is introduced. Think about the language you would use to do this. For further information, see Chapter 17.

Presentation of new language This is designed to show it in context and get across its meaning.

Controlled practice Opportunities for your pupils to practise the new language in carefully controlled activities directed by you.

Production The so-called 'free' stage, in which your pupils have the chance to use the new language relatively spontaneously. This may be in a game or roleplay, for example, and may be oral or written.

Reviewing What have we done today? Another opportunity for pupils to reflect on the lesson and their part in it.

Rounding up A confirmation of the aims of the lesson: *Good. Today we've learnt how to describe people: we played a guessing game when you described a pupil in the class without saying his/her name and your partner had to guess who it was. Don't forget to revise your vocabulary for homework and I'll see you again on Friday at 1.30. Goodbye!*

The above procedures are in no fixed order. It is common for teachers to present new language, then do some practice, then get the pupils to use language more freely. However, a teacher might decide to present a structure, practise it quickly, then present and practise something else before going on to a final production activity. Each stage could occur several times in a single lesson. Procedures may also overlap: listening to a dialogue might be part of the presentation or it might be a quite separate activity; answering questions on a dialogue is part of listening but also gives pupils speaking practice. The different procedures represent the main focus of an activity.

Variety

A lesson also needs variety in terms of:

● types of activity: problem solving, a song, a game, a dialogue, a roleplay, picture dictation, etc.

- types of interaction: teacher and whole class, teacher and individual pupils, pairs, groups.

- language skills: listening, speaking, reading, writing.

- tempo: It is important to vary the pace of a lesson.

Feedback
It is a good idea to include an element, however informal, of testing, in order that both teacher and pupils can assess achievement.

Having given careful thought to all these elements, it would now be possible to complete the procedures page of your lesson planning sheet. See page 154.

After the lesson

Allow some time after the lesson to reflect on what happened in your class. This is helpful for future planning and can build up your self-confidence. Chapter 15 discusses self-assessment in more detail.

Be honest in your self-appraisals. To simply say, 'I think it went well' or 'The lesson was fine' tells you nothing. Probe deeper and ask yourself why.

Self-assessment
Here are some questions you might ask yourself.

- Did I achieve the aims stated on my lesson plan? If not, why not?

- Was my lesson different from my plan in any way? How and why?

- How did I move from one stage of the lesson to the next? What did I say to the class?

- Did I keep to my timing? If not, why not?

- Did my pupils enjoy the lesson? Why, and how do I know?

- Did my pupils learn what I set out to teach? How do I know?

- Were there any problems? If yes, why?

- What would I do differently next time? Why?

- What did I do better this time than ever before?

Here are some further suggestions that you could use from time to time to help in evaluating your lessons.

● Tape- or video-record your lessons.

● Ask your pupils to comment on your lessons.

● If possible, invite a colleague to sit in on a lesson and observe. Afterwards, answer the questions above individually, and then come together and compare your comments.

References and further reading

Rivers, W., 1968. *Teaching Foreign Language Skills*: University of Chicago Press.

13 Using storybooks

This chapter discusses why and how storybooks can be used, offers criteria that can be used when selecting storybooks, suggests techniques that the teacher can use to improve his or her story-telling techniques, and offers guide-lines on how to set up a book corner.

Introducing and exploiting storybooks successfully in the class-room needs careful planning. Simply reading a story aloud to a class without preparation could be disastrous, with a loss of pupil attention, motivation, and self-confidence. To understand a story in a foreign language, pupils will need to feel involved and relate it to aspects of their own experience such as to the area in which they live, the animals with which they are familiar, to the things they like and dislike and so on. This takes gradual preparation which could spread over several lessons. The overall aim of using storybooks is to encourage general comprehension and to trigger off a wealth of purposeful language learning activities.

Why use storybooks?

Children enjoy listening to stories in their mother tongue and understand the conventions of narrative. For example, as soon as they hear the formula, *Once upon a time . . .*, they know what to expect next. For this reason, storybooks can provide an ideal introduction to the foreign language as it is presented in a context that is familiar to the child. Stories can also provide the starting point for a wide variety of related language and learning activities. Here are some further reasons why teachers use storybooks.

1 Stories are motivating and fun and can help develop positive attitudes towards the foreign language and language learning, and create a desire to continue learning.

2 Stories exercise the imagination. Children can become personally involved in a story as they identify with the characters and try to make their own interpretation of the narrative and illustra-tions. This imaginative experience helps them to develop their own creative powers.

3 Stories are a useful tool in linking fantasy and the imagination with the child's real world. They provide a way of enabling children to make sense of their everyday life and forge links between home and school.

4 Listening to stories in class is a shared social experience. Reading and writing are often individual activities; storytelling provokes a shared response of laughter, sadness, excitement and anticipation which is not only enjoyable but can help build up the child's confidence and encourage social and emotional development.

5 Children enjoy listening to stories over and over again. This frequent repetition allows certain language items to be acquired while others are being overtly reinforced. Many stories also contain natural repetition of key vocabulary and structures, for example, the shop keepers and the phrase *Would you like . . .?'* in *The Elephant and the Bad Baby* (see page 166). This helps children to remember every detail so they can gradually learn to anticipate what is about to happen next in the story. Repetition also encourages participation in the narrative, thereby providing a type of 'hidden' pattern practice in a meaningful context. Following meaning and predicting language are important skills in language learning.

6 Having the children listen to stories allows the teacher to revise or introduce new vocabulary and sentence structures by exposing the children to language in varied, memorable, and familiar contexts, which will enrich their thinking and gradually enter their own language production.

7 Listening to stories develops the child's listening and concentrating skills via:
● visual clues, for example, pictures and illustrations
● their prior knowledge of how language works
● their general knowledge.
These help them to understand the overall meaning of a story and relate it to their personal experience.

8 Stories create opportunities for developing continuity in children's learning since they can be chosen to consolidate learning in other school subjects across the curriculum.

9 Learning English through stories can lay the foundations for secondary school in terms of basic language functions and structures, vocabulary, and language learning skills.

Selecting storybooks

Many publishers produce simplified storybooks for children learning English. However, there are many authentic storybooks written for English-speaking children which are also suitable for children learning English. Authentic storybooks are those which have not been written specifically for the teaching of English as a foreign language so the language has not been selected or graded. Many, however, contain language traditionally found in most beginner syllabuses. The advantage of using authentic storybooks is that they provide examples of 'real' language and help to bring the 'real' world into classroom. Very often, simplified stories represent a 'watered down' version of the English language and can deceive both the teacher and the learners about the true nature of language. Authentic storybooks can also be very motivating for a child as they experience a strong sense of achievement at having worked with a 'real' book. Furthermore, the quality of illustrations in these books is usually of a very high standard and very appealing to the young learner and plays an important role in aiding their general comprehension. For further information on selecting and using authentic storybooks see Ellis and Brewster (1991).

Types of storybooks

Teachers can choose from a wide range of storybooks: stories children are already familiar with in their mother tongue, such as traditional tales and fairy tales; picture stories with no text where the children build up the story together; rhyming stories; cumulative stories with predictable endings; humorous stories; stories with infectious rhythms; everyday stories; fantasy stories; animal stories; and so on.

Care needs to be taken, however, when selecting authentic storybooks for children learning English in order to choose those that are accessible, useful and relevant. What criteria, then, can a teacher use? The diagram in Figure 19 breaks down three major objectives of language teaching into criteria which are further translated into questions you could ask yourself. The objectives overlap to some extent, as indicated by the arrows.

Using storybooks – a methodology

Storybooks offer variety and can be used to provide extra language practice by supplementing and complementing another language course. For example, if you have just covered a unit in your coursebook about animals, you may like to read your pupils an animal story. Or, if you have just covered a unit which has introduced a particular language function and structure, you may like to read a story which shows how this language is used in a different context. Using stories in this way makes learning more memorable and fun. Alternatively, if you do not have to adhere rigidly to a particular coursebook, storybooks can also be used as short basic syllabuses in their own right. As many storybooks contain language traditionally found in beginner syllabuses, they can be used to introduce, for the first time, elements of the English language thereby providing a novel alternative to the coursebook.

Although children are used to listening to stories in their mother tongue, understanding a story in a foreign language is hard work. Pupils' enjoyment will increase enormously if we ensure that their understanding is supported in several ways. This takes gradual preparation and the following guide-lines provide a framework you could use to plan story-based lessons.

1 Identify your linguistic objectives. Decide which language points your pupils need to recognize for comprehension when the story is told. Decide which language points would be useful for your pupils to reproduce, such as lexical sets, language functions and structures, and so on.

2 Provide a context for the story and introduce the main characters; help your pupils feel involved and link their experience with that in the story to set the scene, for example, relate it to aspects of their own experience, such as going shopping, having picnics, to people they know, and so on. Once the context has been understood by the children and they can identify with the characters, elicit key vocabulary and phrases and involve them in predicting and participating in the story as much as possible.

3 Explain the context, key words and ideas in the child's mother tongue if necessary.

4 Provide visual support: use of drawings on the blackboard; cut-out figures; speech bubbles; masks; puppets; realia; flash-cards, etc. Can your pupils make any of these?

5 If possible, relate the story or associated activities with work in the other subject areas you are working on with your pupils.

6 Decide how long you will spend using the story. Will you use it once or twice or over a period of several lessons?

7 Decide when you will read the story. Will you read a little each lesson or all at once after appropriate preparation?

8 Decide in which order you are going to introduce or revise the language necessary for understanding the story. Make sure pupils understand the aim of each lesson and how it relates to the story: to learn vocabulary for the different food shops in

Figure 19   Criteria for selecting storybooks

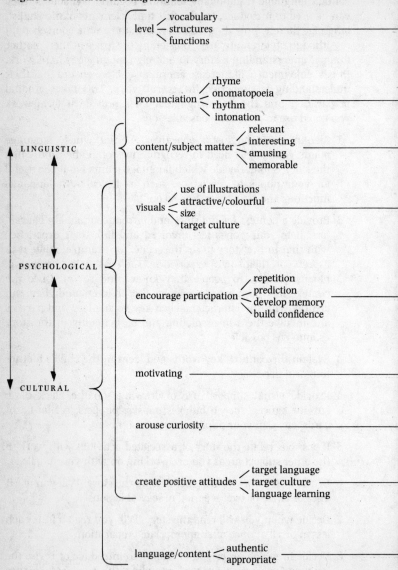

Is the language level appropriate? Not too easy? Not too difficult? Does the story contain language included in beginner syllabuses, for example, vocabulary, structures and functions? Will it provide my pupils with a successful learning experience?

Does the story contain any features such as rhyme, onomatopoeia, rhythm, intonation that my pupils will enjoy imitating and improve their pronunciation?

Will the story interest my pupils? Is it relevant to their needs? Is it amusing? Is it memorable?

Do the illustrations relate to the text and support the children's understanding? Are they appropriate to the age of my pupils? Are they attractive and colourful? Are they big enough for all the class to see? Do they depict life in the target culture?

Is there any natural repetition to encourage participation in the text and to provide pattern practical pronunciation practice; to recycle language items and develop memory skills? Does the repetition allow my pupils to predict what is coming next in the story and to build up their confidence?

Will the story motivate my pupils by drawing on their personal experience? Will it develop their imagination and appeal to their sense of humour?

Will the story arouse their curiosity and make them want to find out more about the target language, culture and language learning?

Will my pupils respond positively to the story and develop positive attitudes towards the target language, culture and towards language learning?

Is the language representative of the variety spoken in the target culture? Does the story provide any information about life in the target culture? Does it contain any obscure cultural references that may be difficult to understand? Is it too culture specific?

EDUCATIONAL POTENTIAL

What is the learning potential of the story in terms of learning about other subjects, the target culture, the world and learning about learning?

POTENTIAL FOR FOLLOW-UP WORK

Does the story provide a starting point for related language activities and lead on to follow-up work such as drama or roleplay in order to reinforce vocabulary and structures in a meaningful and memorable way?

The Elephant and the Bad Baby, for example. Check that each
lesson provides plenty of variety and opportunities for recycling
language previously introduced.

9   If necessary, modify the story to make it more accessible to
    your pupils and easier to follow by substituting unfamiliar
    words with more well-known ones and adapting sentence
    structures, and so on.

10 Find out if there are any rhymes or songs that pupils can learn
    to help reinforce language introduced.

11 Decide which follow-up activities would provide opportunities
    for pupils to produce language from the story in different
    contexts, for example, roleplay, dramatization, creative activi-
    ties, surveys, and so on.

Storytelling techniques

Some stories are available on audio cassette. However, since the
beginning of spoken language and in every civilization, people
have told stories orally. This gives them a breath of life the printed
word or cassette recording cannot always do. For this reason, we
suggest you read the stories aloud as often as possible to your
pupils rather than use a recorded version, and especially the first
time they hear it. This is important for the following reasons:

● It allows you to develop a more personal rapport with your
  pupils and to involve them actively in the story.

● You can help make the story come alive through use of intonation, gesture, mime, and so on, and by making maximum use
  of the illustrations to help convey meaning.

● Reading a story aloud to your pupils yourself is more flexible
  than using a cassette recording as it allows you to anticipate
  when to stop and ask pupils questions so that they can relate
  the story to their own experience. It allows you to repeat a part
  of the story immediately if you sense the pupils have not
  understood, to encourage them to repeat or to predict what
  happens next, to join in, to clarify a language item or cultural
  detail, or to refer to some other work you have covered together.

Using a cassette recording can, however, be beneficial for the
following reasons:

● It provides variety by allowing pupils to hear English spoken by
  someone else other than their teacher, i.e., another voice,
  another accent, and so on.

- The voice on the cassette provides a constant model and provides examples of English as spoken by a native speaker.

- Some recordings contain amusing sound effects which are motivating and can help pupils guess the meanings of unknown words.

- The voice on the cassette provides a model for the teacher to imitate by demonstrating a number of storytelling techniques, such as disguising the voice for different characters, intonation patterns, stress and rhythm, alternation of the pace of the voice, and so on.

However, it is important to bear in mind that playing a cassette recording of a story can become a mechanical activity unless it is exploited in a way that actively involves pupils in listening tasks. The section on learning to listen in Chapter 6 describes a number of while-listening activities, which give you an idea of the different possibilities.

There are a number of techniques you can use when reading stories aloud to make the experience more enjoyable and successful for your pupils. If they are unfamiliar with storytelling, begin with short sessions which do not demand too much from them and stretch their concentration span.

- If possible, have the children sit on the floor around you when you read the story, making sure everyone can see your face and the illustrations in the story.

- Read slowly and clearly. Give your pupils time to think, ask questions, look at the pictures, make comments. However, vary the pace of your voice when the story speeds up.

- Make comments about the illustrations. When you say a word point to the illustration at the same time. Involve your pupils actively by asking pupils to point to the illustrations, and so on.

- Encourage your pupils to participate in the storytelling by repeating key vocabulary items and phrases. You can invite them to do this by pausing and looking at them with a questioning expression and by putting your hand to your ear to indicate that you are waiting for them to join in. The following examples (see Figures 20 and 21) are taken from *The Elephant and the Bad Baby* and *My Cat Likes to Hide in Boxes*. The slashes indicate where you can pause so that your pupils can join in.

- Use gestures, mime, facial expressions, varied intonation, pace and tone, and disguise your voice for different characters as much as possible to help convey meaning and to keep your pupils' attention.

Next they came to a baker's shop.
And the elephant said to the Bad Baby/'Would you like a bun?'
And the Bad Baby said, 'Yes.'
   So the Elephant stretched out his trunk and took a bun for himself
and a bun for the Bad Baby, and they went/rumpeta, rumpeta,
rumpeta, all down the road, with the/ice-cream man, and the/pork
butcher, and the baker all running after.

**Figure 20   Extract from *The Elephant and the Bad Baby*
by Elfrida Vipont and Raymond Briggs**

   As already discussed, pupils enjoy hearing stories over and over
again. Read a story or part of it as often as possible so that your
pupils hear English frequently. If a cassette recording of the story is
available, allow pupils to listen to this when they wish or use it to
reinforce the learning of slower learners.

Evaluating your storytelling techniques

Reading stories aloud is not an easy task and any teacher, whether
a native speaker or not, needs to practise this skill. Use cassette
recordings when possible to provide you with a model to copy. If
you can, rehearse at home or with another colleague, record
yourself and then compare this with the model. This will help you
develop your confidence and to hear which areas need improving.
You may like to use the self-assessment sheet which follows to
evaluate your performance (see Figure 22).

Preparation
1 Familiarize yourself with the book, the story, and illustrations.

The cat from Greece
Joined the police.
The cat from Norway
Got stuck in the/doorway.
The cat from Spain
Flew an/aeroplane.
The cat from France
Liked to/sing and dance.

Figure 21 Extract from *My Cat Likes to Hide in Boxes*
by Eve Sutton and Lynley Dodd

2 Decide where you may wish to pause in the story or invite your pupils to join in.
3 Find a private room where you can record yourself at ease and imagine you are reading the story to your pupils. When you have recorded yourself, listen to your recording and ask yourself the questions on the sheet.

This rehearsal will prepare you for when you read a story aloud to your pupils in the classroom. You may also like to record yourself reading the story in the classroom and use the self-assessment sheet again afterwards.

Self-assessment sheet

1 **Pronunciation.** Did I have any problems with any vowels or consonants?

_____

2 **Stress.** Did I have any problems with stress in individual words or in sentences?

_____

3 **Rhythm.** Did I read too slowly or too quickly? Did I pause in the right places?

_____

4 **Intonation.** Did I sound interesting or boring and did I vary my intonation where appropriate? Did I use the appropriate intonation for questions, statements, lists, and so on?

_____

5 **Variation.** Did I vary the pace and the loudness of my voice where appropriate? Did I disguise my voice enough for the different characters?

_____

6 **Pupil participation.** Did I pause in the correct places and use appropriate intonation to invite my pupils to join it? Did I ask the appropriate questions to encourage my pupils to predict what comes next?

_____

7 **General impression.** How did I sound in general? Clear? Expressive? Lively?

_____

8 **What do I need to improve?** What shall I focus on this week?

_____

Figure 22   Self-assessment questionnaire 3

Organizing a book corner

Most primary school classrooms have a book corner where pupils can look through books of their own choice and at their own pace. Once a story in English has been completed in class, it is a good idea to put extra copies of it in the book corner. This will provide an introduction to the written word in English.

Furthermore, as the children will have memorized much of the story, they will be able to make the connection between what they have heard and memorized and what they see written and illustrated on the page. A stimulating book area will also promote a positive attitude towards reading and create enthusiasm among children for books.

Setting up the book corner
If you do not already have a book corner in your class or would prefer to set up a special one for English, you may find the following tips useful.

- A bookcase or shelving is ideal but a table or cardboard boxes covered in coloured paper can be used to display and store books.

- Flowers, plants, a carpet, cushions will make the book corner cosy, attractive and inviting.

- If possible, display books with the cover showing. This is more attractive and makes selection much easier.

- Try to involve your pupils as much as possible in the organization of the book corner. Looking after a book corner encourages children to take responsibility for the care of books. The class could elect book corner monitors/librarians each week or month whose duties will be to keep the book corner tidy.

- Decorate the corner with any artwork or writing done by the pupils which has been inspired by stories read to them in class. Pupils could also write comments about different books and stick these on the wall. Get the children to organize a Top Ten Books chart and display the results in the corner.

- Bring your pupils' attention to other books in English or in the mother tongue related to a topic you are covering, for example, magic, dinosaurs, butterflies, witches, animals, etc.

If it is feasible, allow pupils to have open access to the book corner. This will encourage them to use it as often as possible without feeling they have to use it at specific times.

If your pupils may borrow the books, you will need to devise a lending system. A simple system is to use an exercise book in which pupils write their name, the title of the books, date borrowed, and date returned. Decide how long the lending period should be: one week, two weeks? The book corner monitors/librarians could take responsibility for this.

It is useful for pupils to keep a personal record of books they

Figure 23 Pupil record cards

(⚇) PENGUIN JEUNESSE (⚇)

Class Library – Pupil Record Card

Name _____   Class _____

Title/author	Date borrowed	Date returned	Comments	Title/Author	Date borrowed	Date returned	Comments

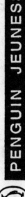

PENGUIN JEUNESSE

Class Library — Pupil Record Card

Name _____

Class _____

Title/author	Date borrowed	Date returned	Type of book	Problems	Useful vocabulary and information	Comments

have looked through or borrowed (see Figure 23). You could design a record card which enables them to do this. The amount of detail you include will depend on the age, level, and interests of your pupils, but noting down even basic information will help pupils learn useful study skills. The information recorded can be written in English or in the mother tongue.

Effective organization and imaginative display of your book corner both play a vital role in helping your pupils develop a positive attitude towards books, reading and the foreign language.

Similarly, you could provide a poster to keep a class record of books read. You will need a large sheet of paper. Write the titles of books horizontally and the names of your pupils vertically to form a grid. This can be designed by the pupils themselves. When they have read a book, they put a tick in the corresponding box. At the end of a school term or year, pupils can collate the results:

8 pupils read 'The Very Hungry Caterpillar'
10 pupils read 'Meg on the Moon'

and so on.

The most popular book was . . . .

Associated activities
There are several activities which can follow on very naturally from regular book reading.

DRAWING AND COLOURING
Children love drawing and the titles included in the book corner will provide them with ideal models for their drawings. They can redraw the characters, create maps showing where the story takes place, think of other possible cover illustrations, and so on.

The results of their efforts can be kept and then used as collages or posters to decorate appropriate areas of the book corner. Alternatively, each pupil could put together a folder of his/her own work.

HANDICRAFTS
Bearing in mind the limitations of time and space, pupils can be encouraged to create their own masks, hats, and other props, as well as models of streets and buildings etc., inspired by the characters, and places they have encountered in the books they have enjoyed.

Activities of this kind present an ideal opportunity for developing oral comprehension through the language used for giving instructions.

SONGS AND RHYMES

Very often, the themes developed in stories are to be found in various songs and rhymes. Learning such songs and rhymes provides an opportunity for pupils to practise, through imitation and repetition, the rhythm and intonation of the English language – and to enjoy themselves at the same time. See Chapter 14 on the use of games, songs and rhymes for further suggestions on how they can be exploited.

VOCABULARY ACTIVITIES

Pupils can create their own 'Picture Dictionary', based on words from the stories they have read or heard. They can work individually or pool their efforts to illustrate the words, either by drawing pictures themselves or by cutting pictures out of magazines or catalogues. They can choose whether to arrange the words alphabetically or thematically (for example, animals, the weather, shops, food, etc.). For further suggestions, see Chapter 8 on learning English vocabulary.

References and further reading

Dunn, O., 1984. *Developing English with Young Learners*: Macmillan.

Ellis, G. and J. Brewster, 1991. *The Storytelling Handbook for Primary Teachers*: Penguin English.

Garvie, E., 1990. *Story as Vehicle*: Multilingual Matters.

Hedge, T., 1985. *Using Readers in Language Teaching*: Macmillan.

Hestor, H., 1983. *Stories in the Multilingual Primary Classroom*: Harcourt Brace Jovanovich.

Sutton E., and L. Dodd, 1978. *My Cat Likes to Hide in Boxes*: Puffin.

Vipont, E. and R. Briggs, 1971. *The Elephant and the Bad Baby*: Puffin.

14   Using games, songs and rhymes

Every primary school teacher will know how much children enjoy
games and music. These activities provide a link with home and
school life and are often lively and fun. Their usefulness is recognized by their adoption as common language learning activities
which frequently form an integral part of language programmes
and published ELT materials for children.

Why use games, songs and rhymes?

Here is a list of some of their advantages for language learning
purposes. You might like to put two ticks in the boxes for those
you think are very important, one tick for those you think are
quite important and a cross by those you think are not important
in your teaching context.

Advantages of using games, songs and rhymes	Yes or No
1 Variety is added to the range of learning situations.	
2 The pace of a lesson can be changed, thus maintaining pupils' motivation.	
3 More formal teaching can be 'lightened', thus renewing pupils' energy.	
4 'Hidden' practice of specific language patterns, vocabulary and pronunciation can be provided.	
5 Listening skills, attention span and concentration are improved.	
6 Pupil participation is encouraged, thereby giving confidence to shy pupils.	
7 Pupil–pupil communication is increased, which provides fluency practice and reduces the domination of the class by the teacher.	
8 Any distance between teacher and pupils can be reduced by the use of more light-hearted and 'fun' activities.	
9 Areas of weakness and the need for further language work can be revealed.	

Types of songs and rhymes

Songs and rhymes for the learning of English can be divided into at least four types:

- action songs and rhymes
- limericks, humorous verse and riddles
- traditional songs and rhymes
- 'pop' songs.

Action songs and rhymes

Skipping, dipping, counting and finger rhymes can all be included in this category, as well as other songs which can be accompanied by actions. Many skipping rhymes are traditionally used by children to perform actions while they skip in groups. Here is an example (the most strongly-stressed words are in bold type).

EXAMPLE A

*Teddy bear, teddy bear, **touch the ground**,*   [*touch floor*]

*Teddy bear, teddy bear, **turn around**,*   [*turn*]

*Teddy bear, teddy bear, **walk upstairs**,*   [*climb stairs*]

*Teddy bear, teddy bear, **say your prayers**,*   [*fold hands*]

*Teddy bear, teddy bear, **turn** out the **light**,*   [*turns out light*]

*Teddy bear, teddy bear, **say good**night.*   [*leaves the rope*]

Dipping rhymes or 'dips' are a kind of counting rhyme. They are used to eliminate children when deciding who is going to be a key person for a game (for example, the chaser in a chasing game, usually referred to as 'it'). The children hold out their fists and the 'counter' touches each fist on every stressed syllable. When a person is 'out', it means they are eliminated and will not be 'it'. Here are two examples:

EXAMPLE B

Eenery Meenery Minery Mo

*Tickle your **tummy** and tickle your **toe***

*If you **laugh** then **out** you **go***

*and **that means you***

(If a child laughs s/he drops out.)

EXAMPLE C

Each peach pear plum

Who's your best chum

*Not to be on '**it**'*

(The last child left will be 'it'.)

Finger rhymes involve actions just for the hand, such as this one:

EXAMPLE D

Two little **monkeys** *fighting in* **bed**	(use 2 fingers)
One *fell* **out** *and* **hurt** *his* **head**	(hand on head)
The **other** *called the* **doctor**	(mime dialling)
And the **doctor said**	(open and close palm)
That *is what you* **get** *for* **fighting in bed**	(wag finger)

Once some of these rhymes have been learned, you will probably find the children practising them in the playground. Action songs and rhymes are useful if the children are feeling particularly restless. Finger rhymes can be used with the children sitting in their seats, while other songs, such as *If you're happy and you know it . . .*, which require more vigorous actions, are better if the children are standing up or moving around. The last example is of a rather boisterous action song where the children mime the actions as they sing.

EXAMPLE E

1 *The* **wheels** *on the* **bus** *go* **round** *and* **round**,
   round *and* **round**, **round** *and* **round**,
   The **wheels** *on the* **bus** *go* **round** *and* **round**,
   all day long.

2 The **wipers** *on the* **bus** *go* **swish swish swish** etc.

3 The **driver** *on the* **bus** *goes* **'Toot! Toot! Toot!'** etc.

4 The **con**ductor *on the* **bus** *says* **'Hurry please!'** etc.

5 The **people** *on the* **bus** *go* '**yakkity-yak**' etc.

6 *The* **children** *on the* **bus** *make* **too much noise!** etc.

7 *The* **babies** *on the* **bus** *fall* **fast asleep** etc.

Limericks, humorous verse and riddles

Riddles not only practise language but also encourage the children to think. Can you answer these?

EXAMPLE F
You eat me for breakfast
But first crack my shell
If I'm fresh then I'm tasty
If not – what a smell!

EXAMPLE G
I'm a very big animal
You see at the zoo
I've a very nice trunk
I can squirt water through

Limericks are also very popular with older children:

EXAMPLE H
There once was a man from Darjeeling,
Who travelled from London to Ealing
When it said on the door
'Please don't spit on the floor',
He carefully spat on the ceiling.

Traditional and pop songs

Traditional songs are often very popular although older children might find some of these a little childish or uninteresting. In this case, teachers often use English 'pop' songs, especially some of the 'classics' such as those of The Beatles. If you look at some record albums, the words are often printed inside. Otherwise, you could listen with the children to work them out.

You might choose songs and rhymes to fit in with certain grammatical patterns you are teaching or to fit in with a topic or story you are teaching. There are, for example, several songs and rhymes relating to the topics of animals, the weather, colours, and so on. Make sure that the words of rhymes are not too archaic or too childish for the age group of the class. Also check that the rhyme does not force the speaker to produce an unnatural rhythmic pattern. Limericks, for example, often start with this pattern:

There <u>was</u> a young man from Darjeeling . . .

The rhythmic pattern forces the speaker to put the stress on *was*, which is very inauthentic. By adding the word *once* and deleting *young*, you overcome this problem:

There <u>once</u> was a man from Darjeeling . . .

How to use songs and rhymes

Songs and rhymes are useful for practising new grammatical patterns or vocabulary once they have been presented. This can be done with the use of drawings on the board, mime or explanations in the mother tongue. The rhymes or songs can be sung by the whole class, or you may like to vary the groupings, so that if there is a question and answer sequence in the song (such as *There's a Hole in my Bucket*), one part can be sung by half the class, the second part by the other half.

Songs and rhymes are particularly useful for practising pronunciation. This includes individual sounds and sounds in connected speech but, more importantly, features relating to stress, rhythm and intonation. For more details on pronunciation, see Chapter 8.

Individual sounds and sounds in connected speech

Many vowels and certain consonants in English provide pronunciation difficulties. Some individual sounds can be demonstrated through animal noises or by explaining what should be happening with the tongue, lips and teeth. For instance, *Example A* is good for practising the sounds /eə/, /əʊ/ and /aɪ/.

Songs and rhymes are useful for showing what happens to sounds in connected speech, for example, the way that certain sounds run on together:

Example A: turn around

  walk upstairs

  turn out the light

Example C: not to be on it

Rather complicated consonant clusters in English are often simplified, especially where a word which ends in /t/ or /d/ is followed by a consonant cluster, as in:

Example C: Who's your best chum?

  where /st/ + /tʃ/ are simplified to /s/ + /tʃ/

Stress and rhythm

More important features of pronunciation, such as stress and rhythm, can also be practised in a very natural way using songs and rhymes. This is particularly important for learners of languages like French, which is a 'syllable-timed' language, i.e. each syllable is stressed almost equally. English, by contrast, is a 'stress-timed' language where stressed syllables tend to occur at regularly spaced intervals. Encouraging children to clap the beat as they sing or say rhymes will help to develop a sense of rhythm in English.

Weak forms, where the pronunciation of a word differs according to whether it is stressed or unstressed, occur regularly in songs and rhymes. The words which are weakly stressed include auxiliary verbs, conjunctions, the articles, prepositions, and some pronouns:

Example C: *not to be on it*	/tə/
Example D: *and the doctor said*	/ən/ /ðə/
Example F: *you eat me for breakfast*	/jʊ/ /mɪ/ /fə/
what a smell	/ə/

These weak forms often practise the use of /ə/, which is the most frequent vowel in English since it occurs in many unstressed syllables. This is usually not a difficult vowel to pronounce but learners often find it difficult to know when it occurs.

Intonation
Intonation can also be practised in rhymes. Chapter 8 described the use of falling tones for short statements, *wh-* questions, commands and exclamations, and the rising tone for requests, statements turned into questions, Yes/No questions and clauses occurring before the main verb.

Ear training
Chapter 8 referred to the need for pupils to have some 'ear-training' to help them distinguish between different aspects of English pronunciation. To do this, you can ask the pupils to listen and count how many times an individual sound or word occurs in a song or rhyme. You can also ask the pupils to listen and discriminate by checking whether rhythmic or intonation patterns are the same or different. Rhythmic patterns can be presented visually by using large and small circles or boxes, for example:

Insey Winsey Spider	O o O o O o
Climbing up the spout	O o O o O
Down came the rain and	O O o O o
Washed the spider out	O o O o O

Integrating songs with other activities

We have seen how songs and rhymes can be used to practise fluency, especially pronunciation skills. The children are also developing listening skills which at the same time can lead to reading and writing practice (usually for older children). Some while-listening activities include:

● Listen and fill in the blanks
  Useful for longer 'pop' songs; provide the words but leave a few gaps for children to complete.

● Listen and sequence
  Individually or in pairs, children scan written phrases and put them in order.

● Listen and sort
  Children have the words from two songs mixed up together. As they listen, they sort out the captions into two piles.

Children might like to make a class book of favourite songs or rhymes. Older ones might also like to produce their own material, such as limericks, which have a very clear rhyming pattern, or their own songs. These could be taped for other children to listen to and to complete the above activities.

There are many books containing songs and rhymes suitable for young learners. Some published coursebooks also include examples and cassettes of songs. Details of these can be found in the section on teachers' books in the Appendix.

Games

There are many different kinds of games, which can be grouped under three headings. These headings include those which relate to the overall purpose of the game; the different groupings required to play the game; the resources required or the language items or skills practised.

The purpose of playing games

Games can be divided into 'code-control games' or 'communication games'. The former aim to practise new language items and develop accuracy, often taking the form of hidden drills. The purpose is usually to score more points than others and there is often a clear 'winner'. An example of this kind of game is 'I went to market and I bought . . .' Here the class has to remember and repeat in the correct order a set of items bought in a market, for example:

1st child: I went to market and I bought a kilo of grapes.
2nd child: I went to market and I bought a kilo of grapes and a
                    packet of sweets.
                    etc.

The child (or team) who remembers most items in the correct order is the winner. Through constant repetition, this game provides practice in the irregular past tense of *buy* and vocabulary items connected with food and quantities.

'Communication games', on the other hand, tend to move away from a focus on accuracy to the development of fluency and more purposeful 'communication'. These games often rely on an 'information gap', where one child has information that the other child needs in order to achieve something, for example, to complete a practical task such as following instructions to make a model or drawing. An example of a communication game is Describe and Arrange, where one child makes a pattern while the second child tries to reproduce the pattern without seeing the original. This requires the children to use their knowledge of appropriate language, such as the vocabulary of shapes and colours, prepositional phrases, and different ways of negotiating meaning, such as asking questions, asking for clarification, or explaining. In this game, the children are expected to draw upon any of their linguistic resources to complete the task, and it is therefore at a higher level of sophistication than many 'code-control' games. 'Code-control' games are more likely to be played with the whole class or teams, while 'communication' games are often played in pairs or small groups.

Resources required

Games can be classified by the resources required to play them. Some, such as I-spy or Simon Says, rely on talk and listening and require no resources. They are often based on riddles or on providing an appropriate response involving activity. Others, such as Consequences or Hangman, are 'pencil and paper' games, which can often be presented to the whole class using the blackboard. Some games, like Dominoes or Bingo, need cards with pictures or words; these might include matching exercises or other problem-solving activities. Less common are 'board games' which need a board, dice and counters, with 'chance' cards. An example, called The Five Senses Game, has a board with pictures of different items and 'chance' cards with instructions such as 'If you can smell this, move on two spaces' or 'If you cannot eat this, move back four spaces' and so on. This practises the first conditional tense, verbs to describe the five senses, vocabulary items of the pictures, and reading skills.

Language practised

There are many games which focus on speaking only, such as practising new vocabulary or specific tenses; others focus on listening skills, for example, Simon Says. Some games, like Hangman, are particularly useful for developing spelling, while Consequences is good for practising writing simple sentences. Reading skills are practised in games like Synonym Bingo or Jumbled Sayings, where players match or sequence words.

How to play games

We have already seen some of the advantages of using games. This means that they can be used at different stages in a lesson, not always at the end. They can, for example, begin a lesson in a lively and stimulating way, relieve tension after a test, punctuate a more formal lesson when interest is flagging, or give the class an opportunity to be active if the pupils are feeling restless.

Many of the games that children play in their mother tongue can be used for learning English: Simon Says, What's the time Mr. Wolf?, Bingo, and Dominoes, for example. You can probably think of many more. Making use of these games has the advantage that the children already know how to play them. When playing a game which is unfamiliar to the children, however, you will probably need to go through the following stages.

SELECTING, PREPARING AND STORING GAMES

The game you choose may practise certain word families, specific language patterns, or skills, such as listening or spelling. It may also relate to a topic you are working on, such as food and shopping. You will therefore have to decide whether the children need to practise this language using a code-control game, or whether they are ready to use a communication game. If the latter, they must be familiar with the key vocabulary and language patterns and must be able to ask for clarification and so on. Whatever the choice of game, it must then be thoroughly prepared. If written or visual resources are required, these need to be collected or made beforehand (the children could help with any drawings or copying). You might have the games stored in envelopes in the classroom, in which case setting up the game is easier if they are labelled and colour- or shape-coded. An example of how you might do this is shown in the chart on page 183. The games referred to are described in Carrier et al. (1980)

Bear in mind that it may be wise to vary the choice of games so that there is not always a competitive element; communication games focus on co-operation and are more likely to give every

Organizing and storing games		
A Games to practise language items		
		CIRCLES
adjectives	green	Describe it
verbs	red	Yesterday Afternoon
B Games to practise writing and spelling:		
		STARS
spelling	blue	Word pyramids
wordbuilding	yellow	Word ladders

child a chance to have a turn to speak in an unthreatening atmosphere. As we saw in Chapter 6, an overly competitive atmosphere in the classroom can be demoralizing for some children.

GIVING INSTRUCTIONS

This is a crucial stage; the teacher must ensure that very clear instructions are given before and during the game. You will probably do this in the mother tongue. Always try to give a demonstration, using any necessary resources and one or two of the children.

ORGANIZING THE CLASS

If the game requires teams, groups or pairs this needs to be organized quickly. It is best if the class becomes familiar with a routine to minimize disruption when moving furniture, collecting the games, forming groups and so on. It is often useful to have a group leader if you want to play games in groups. This pupil will be responsible for collecting equipment, sharing it out, explaining details to the group, putting equipment away. Make sure that the role of group leader is given to different pupils so that they can all take a turn.

PLAYING THE GAME

If you have chosen a code-control game, it is likely that you have a key role in the game. If you are using pairs or groups, however, use the opportunity to monitor the groups, noting the pupils' language use or difficulties. You may like to teach older children the English for *I don't know* or *It's your turn*, and so on. Try not to over-correct the children if this is likely to spoil the flow of the game or dampen their enthusiasm. Make a note of how long the game takes to play for future reference and whether you need to improve on the instruction-giving stage. You will soon find out from the children which games really work!

References and further reading

Carrier, M. et al., 1980. *Take 5: Games and activities for the language learner*: Harrap.

Dakin, J., 1968. *Songs and rhymes for the teaching of English: Teacher's Book*: Longman.

Lee, W., 1986. *Language teaching games and contests* (3rd edition): Oxford University Press.

Retter, C. and N. Valls, 1984. *Bonanza: 77 English language games for young learners*: Longman.

Rixon, S., 1980. *Fun with English*: Macmillan.

Rixon, S., 1991. *The role of fun and games activities in teaching young learners*, in Brumfit, C. et al. (eds) *Teaching English to Children*: Collins.

Part 4   Brushing up your English

15   Self-assessment

The teaching profession can be a solitary one and teachers often complain of feeling isolated. The supportive atmosphere experienced at teacher training college or university and the regular contact with fellow teacher trainees and tutors, discussion and feedback may seem long ago. Teachers are also busy people with tight schedules and responsibilities for many pupils, and often find it difficult to find the time and ways of maintaining and improving their English. In-service teacher training provision, where you can meet other colleagues, brush up your English, and find out about new materials and teaching techniques may be rare. Indeed, teachers are very much on their own! How, then, can they improve their language skills by themselves? The key to self-improvement is to develop your self-awareness, in other words, to learn to judge your own language skills and teaching critically. This can be done through regular self-assessment and introspection.

Self-assessment involves planning what you are going to do, reviewing your plans, carrying out your plans and evaluating your performance. This knowledge will enable you to identify your strong and weak points in order to make future plans for your learning and self-improvement by identifying what you need to work on next. The results of your self-assessment can also help you decide whether what you are doing is effective for you.

Self-assessment in this chapter covers:

English for general purposes. This refers to your personal needs for English, for example, listening to the radio, watching films in English, communicating in English, reading for pleasure, writing English, and so on.

English in the classroom. This refers to the English you use with your pupils in the classroom, such as giving instructions, praising, disciplining, explaining, and so on. Chapter 17 lists some of the common language functions you could use.

Self-assessment concerning your actual teaching performance is covered in Chapter 12 on lesson planning.

English for general purposes

Many teachers complain that they find it difficult to maintain their level of English, due to lack of time, teaching low-level classes, or lack of contact with English-speaking people or materials. Practical ideas and suggestions for improving your English are provided in Chapter 16. However, before deciding how you can improve your English, it is important to identify your needs and wants, the areas that need improving and the time you have available to do this.

Needs and wants

Maria is a primary school teacher in Valencia. She uses English for the following reasons:

'I love going to the cinema to see films in English. I also try to make one trip a year to an English-speaking country to practise my spoken English.'

Think about how you use English.

Areas to improve

Maria then analysed carefully what she feels she can do well and the areas that need improving by completing the following chart (Figure 24).

Situation	OK	Needs improving
Watching films in English	General understanding OK	Understanding • different accents • idiomatic expressions
Listening to native speakers	No problem making myself understood. In fact, people often comment on how good my English is.	• understanding replies • idiomatic expressions • cultural references • different accents

Figure 24   Use of English analysis chart

By thinking about her English in this way, Maria can see clearly which areas need improving. She can now think about how to do this. Chapter 16 describes the strategies she uses.

Time available

Before deciding how you are going to improve your English, it is important to be realistic about the amount of time you can spend on your English. There is no point in setting yourself ambitious aims if, in reality, you do not have the time to devote to achieving them! Lack of progress will only result in demotivation. In order to avoid disappointment, first decide how long you are willing and able to spend per week on your English. The chart below (Figure 25) will help you assess this.

Try to calculate the approximate amount of time you spend doing the following things in a typical week.

Activity	Time (approx.)
Sleeping	
Getting up	
Shopping	
Preparing and eating meals	
Your routine time at school	
Travel to and from school	
Preparation for school	
Marking	
Total time	
How much time does this give you for working on your English in a typical week?	
Is it more or less than you expected?	
If less, are there any activities you could give up or spend less time doing?	
How is the amount of time available to you going to affect your language learning? Are you being realistic about what you can achieve?	

(Adapted from *Autonomy and Foreign Language Learning*, H. Holec, Pergamon 1981, pages 35–7)

Figure 25   Time available for English learning chart

English in the classroom

The English you use in the classroom will be very different from the English you use for general purposes and for your own personal needs. Teachers of young beginners need to think carefully about the language relevant to the needs of young learners. We saw in the section on learning English vocabulary in Chapter 8 that child-centred topics such as toys, games, animals and so on, may require learning new specific vocabulary. Chapter 17 lists a range of common language functions and basic metalanguage you can use in the classroom as well as tips on how to use it.

In order to identify your needs and the areas you need to improve, we suggest you follow the same steps as in 1.

Needs and wants

Think of a young beginners class you teach regularly. Do you speak

- mainly in English?
- mainly in the pupils' mother tongue?
- a mixture of the two?

Why?

Ideally, we should aim for the first of these and this is discussed in further detail in Chapter 17. However, do not feel you must use English all the time. There are certain occasions when it can be useful to use your pupils' language. How much English you use will, of course, depend on the level of your class and how long they have been learning English, the type of activity they are involved in, and your own confidence and language ability. Can you think of some of the reasons for attempting to use mainly English in the classroom? Make a list. Note down also occasions when you would choose to use the pupils' language.

Here are some suggestions for your list:

REASONS FOR USING ENGLISH

- It provides opportunities for pupils to see how English is used for a variety of different purposes, for example, giving instructions, praising, socializing, playing games, and so on, as well as providing opportunities to hear and use real, natural English.

- If you speak mainly in English, it will encourage your pupils to reply in English. This provides practice in listening and speaking and will help them pick up words and expressions beyond the language of the coursebook.

- It helps pupils become aware that English is a language which is used for real communication and not just another school subject.

REASONS FOR USING THE MOTHER TONGUE

- To explain the meaning of a word that the pupils cannot guess from contextual or visual clues. In such cases, it can be quicker to explain in the mother tongue and it avoids interrupting the rhythm of the class.

- To set the scene when using storybooks and to encourage pupils to predict what happens next in a story. For further details on using storybooks, see Chapter 13.

- To carry out those learning to learn activities which require pupils to reflect on their learning or the language. The type of questions the teacher would ask may be beyond the child's comprehension in the target language. For further details on learning to learn, see Chapter 9.

- To explain a cultural reference and to discuss similarities and differences between life in the pupils' country and life in other English-speaking countries.

Areas to improve
Think of the same class again. What problems, if any, do you or your pupils have? Why? Take a look at the way two teachers approached this.

'I try to use English as much as possible in my classes but sometimes the pupils have difficulty in understanding. I'm not sure why!'

(Marie-Thérèse, Toulouse, France)

'I have problems finding the appropriate phrases for social English and
I don't feel I sound spontaneous in
class.'

(Giovanni, Verona, Italy)

Marie-Thérèse and Giovanni used the following technique to analyse their classroom English.

RECORDING YOURSELF

Make a cassette recording of part of one of your lessons (a ten-
minute extract is sufficient). Before listening, decide which area(s)
you are going to focus on, for example,

- English for social chit chat
- Introducing the lesson
- Organizing the pupils
- Presenting new language
- Checking understanding
- Asking questions
- Setting up an activity
- Reviewing
- Ending a lesson
- Other

Do not focus on more than one or two areas at a time. Listen to
your recording and identify any problem areas.

- Marie-Thérèse.
  'I focused on organizing the pupils and asking questions. I now
  realize why my pupils were having difficulty understanding my
  English. For example, for organizing the pupils, I used phrases
  like. "Now, let me see, I would like Benjamin to sit with Mary
  over there". I made the instructions unnecessarily complicated
  and used too much language beyond the children's comprehension so the main message was hidden. I now try to limit my

language and make it more direct, for example, "Benjamin, sit with Mary", "Meddy and Bobby, stand up". When I asked questions, again I made these too complicated. For example, showing the pupils a picture, I would ask, "Now, what can you see in the picture here?" I now ask more direct questions and point clearly to what I am referring to: "Who's this?" "What's this?" etc. Of course, gesture is very important too in helping the pupils understand.'

● Giovanni
'I focused on using social language. My impressions were confirmed! I'm lacking the appropriate language for social chit chat and because of this I don't have the confidence to act spontaneously when a situation arises naturally, such as a book falling off a table. I'm going to learn a number of phrases and questions for social chit chat and practise them until I feel confident. I'm also going to make every effort to react to spontaneous situations. I'll react very simply to begin with and will not worry too much about being totally accurate. When the book fell off the table, I could have said, "Whoops!" or "Oh! Pick it up Andrew!" Instead, I let the occasion pass.'

Try to use this technique regularly and focus on different areas. It can also help you understand the reasons for some of the problems your pupils may be having. Label and date your cassettes. This will enable you to compare them later and you can hear the progress you and your pupils have made.

TIME AVAILABLE
Use the chart on page 187 (Figure 25) to calculate the time you have available to improve your English in the classroom.

16 Improving your language skills

As we saw in Chapter 15, most teachers find it difficult to maintain and improve their language skills. The areas they wish to improve will probably be very specific and differ from teacher to teacher depending on their needs and wants. However, one characteristic that most are likely to have in common is that, despite hard work, they often find it very difficult to perceive any progress. They have reached what is often called a plateau in their learning. This can be very frustrating and can result in a loss of motivation and the willingness to devote further time to language learning. It is crucial to analyse what your strong and weak points are so you can identify which areas you need to improve, and set yourself manageable sub-goals. This will help you channel your time and energy in the right direction and see the progress you are making.

Decide which areas you need or what to improve by assessing your own language skills and calculating how much time you are able to spend on your English, as suggested in Chapter 15.

This chapter provides information about resources for learning English, practical ideas and suggestions for improving your English, as well as some activities related to listening, speaking, reading and writing that you may like to try out yourself. First let us consider what makes a good language learner.

The good language learner

In the 1970s a number of studies were carried out to produce inventories of the characteristics and learning strategies of good language learners. Although each learner develops strategies and techniques which suit his or her own individual needs and personality and implements these in different ways, the findings do allow certain generalizations to emerge which are useful for any learner at any stage in their learning to bear in mind. Ellis and Sinclair (1989) have summarized these characteristics and strategies into seven broad categories. Would any of these categories be useful for you to develop in order to improve your own learning? If so, think about how you could do this.

Good language learners are:

- **self-aware**
  They are aware of, and understand the reasons for, their attitudes and feelings towards language learning and themselves as language learners.

● **inquisitive and tolerant**
They are interested in finding out more about how the language works and how they can apply this knowledge to help them learn more effectively. They are prepared to accept differences between their mother tongue and the target language and to tolerate ambiguity and uncertainty.

● **self-critical**
They assess themselves and monitor their progress regularly.

● **realistic**
They realize that it takes a lot of hard work and time to learn a foreign language and set themselves realistic, manageable short-term aims to make their learning easier to manage and to see their progress. This can also help them to remain motivated.

● **willing to experiment**
They are willing to try out different learning strategies and practice activities and choose those that suit them best.

● **actively involved**
They actively involve themselves in language learning and have sufficient confidence not to mind experimenting with the language and taking risks.

● **organized**
They organize their time and materials in ways which suit them personally and fully exploit the language learning resources available to them inside and outside the classroom.

There may be other categories you would like to add to this list. The important thing is to be clear of your own language learning needs and to think of ways you can achieve them.

Resources for learning English

Before you start thinking about ways to improve your English, it is useful to find out about the resources you have access to where you live. For example:

RADIO
There is almost certainly an English language radio station you can tune into. Whether you prefer to listen to pop songs in English, quiz shows, interviews, current affairs programmes, and so on, find out what programmes are on and when so you can organize your listening. Even having the radio on in the background at home will help you pick up useful cultural information and vocabulary.

Write to BBC English for information about their broadcasts: BBC English, British Broadcasting Corporation, Bush House, PO Box 76, Strand, London WC2B 4PH. Programmes include business English, English grammar and usage, literary criticism, current affairs, soap opera, pop music, and a series which teaches English via the world of cinema and films. There is also a magazine programme, *Speaking of English*, for teachers of English. *BBC English*, a bi-monthly magazine, includes information on times and frequencies as well as home study sections, articles on grammar, usage and literature. Subscription details can be obtained by writing to BBC English, PO Box 96, Cambridge, England.

LONDON CALLING
This is the programme journal of the BBC World Service. It contains a guide to the current recommended transmission times and frequencies for your area. For a free copy and subscription form, write to London Calling, PO Box 76, Bush House, Strand, London WC2B 4PH.

TELEVISION
Films in English are often shown in English on television. Find out when these are.

CABLE TELEVISION
Channels in English include BBC World Service for British English and many other varieties of English, CNN for American English, MTV for pop music and video clips and Eurosport. Soap operas and situational comedies are useful for hearing different varieties of spoken English (*EastEnders* for Cockney English for example) as well as helping you pick up cultural references.

Use TV guides to plan your viewing. Keep a viewing diary.

CINEMA/FILMS/VIDEOS
Find out where you can see films in English, such as your local cinema, at cultural centres, English clubs and so on. Can you borrow video cassettes in English from libraries?

CONFERENCES/TALKS/DISCUSSIONS/DEBATES
It is often possible to listen to native speakers at such events. Contact cultural centres or embassies for information. Join associations for teachers of English. See the Appendix for useful addresses.

ENGLISH CLUBS
Can you join an English club where you can meet other people and have conversations in English and so on?

LIBRARIES

Are there any libraries you can join to borrow reading or listening material in English or English language teaching materials?

SHOPS

Where can you buy newspapers, magazines, books, and so on in English?

COURSES

Find out about language courses or courses for teachers of English either in your country or abroad. See the Appendix for further details.

DICTIONARIES AND GRAMMARS

Equip yourself with a good dictionary and a good grammar book. See the Appendix for suggestions. When selecting a grammar book, think of a grammar point. Can you find it easily? Do you understand the explanation? Are examples of how it is used provided?

Listening

We saw in Chapter 15 that Maria needs to improve certain aspects of her listening comprehension in order to understand films in English.

Here is a strategy she has developed. She felt that if she found out as much as she could about a film before she went to see it, this would prepare her for some of the different accents and idiomatic expressions she might hear.

She decided to read film reviews (like the one in Figure 26), when possible in English, before seeing a film. She found she was able to extract key information about the type of film, its setting, who the main characters were as well as a summary of the storyline. First, she would do this by completing a chart like the one on page 198 (Figure 27). After doing this a few times in detail, she then found she only needed to make a list of these points in her mind. This preparation gave her clues about the style of language to expect in the film.

The chart she completed after having read the review about *Who Framed Roger Rabbit* is on page 196 (Figure 27).

RUN RABBIT

Who Framed Roger Rabbit

JOHN PYM

Hollywood, 1947. Roger Rabbit is a foolish 'Toon'. He lives with the other Toons – Goofy, the Dwarfs, the three Blue Birds, the whole gang, as far as one can judge – in 'Toontown', a ghetto into which real folk only reluctantly venture. The Toons are a sort of despised ethnic minority: feckless, unpredictable, alien. In the real world, the world of you and me, where one is liable to glimpse the immortal Dumbo floating past the office window, humanity goes about its customary business: film studios are swallowed up; private eyes are down on their luck; barmaids wait patiently for their men.

Who Framed Roger Rabbit (Warners) proposes a fantastical but simple notion, that cartoon characters are no more than actors who walk offset at the end of a day's work. The success of the film, the live action directed by Roger Zemeckis and the animation by Richard Williams, springs principally from two sources: the gusto with which the performers, notably Bob Hoskins, as detective Eddie Valiant, interact with the Toons, and the seamlessness with which the live action and animation are integrated.

The picture opens with a delightful cartoon which, in pace and inventiveness, seems to assert that while the old masters to whom the sequence pays tribute were good, their pupils are equally adept. Roger – popeyed, long-eared and with a foolish spotted bow-tie – babysits an infant who soon makes a break from his playpen. The kitchen into which Baby Herman crawls turns out to be a Vietnam jungle of booby traps for the anxious rabbit who scuttles after him. The disasters reach a crescendo, but then an offscreen voice calls a halt, the camera pulls back and the cartoon kitchen is revealed to be a workaday set. Herman, despite his nappy and kiss curl, is an irascible pro – a miniature Mr Magoo – who promptly demands a cigar. Roger himself, it turns out, is a highly-strung crybaby.

The speed and cunning with which the movie's premise is established allows no time for doubts, and the convention once established is readily accepted. From then on, the two worlds intermingle with an easy, unostentatious fluidity. At one point, Eddie and the Rabbit find themselves handcuffed together; the bad hats arrive and Roger is plunged for safety into Eddie's washing-up water. At another, still handcuffed to his protector, the rabbit buffets away under the private eye's trenchcoat. Not spectacular perhaps, but singularly arresting.

Acting with Toons demands special caution, and in this respect Hoskins pitches his performance dead right. He treats the rabbit like a spoilt, fractious child (in short, like an actor), but never makes the mistake of trying to upstage him. Christopher Lloyd, who plays the villain, Judge Doom, is an equally accomplished character actor (he was the boffin in Zemeckis' previous fantasy, *Back to the Future*): his speciality, however, is wide-eyed crazies, not psychopaths but superannuated hippies who are now themselves a bona fide species of likeable cartoon characters. In their different registers, both actors have the temperament to act with animated creatures; they also have the resilience to stand up to their anarchic versatility.

Roger Rabbit's weakness is its plot, a somewhat ponderous attempt to conjure up the spirit of postwar Hollywood detective stories. Most adults don't have the patience to untangle the plot of *The Big Sleep*, and one cannot imagine many seven-year-olds having much patience with this one. Studio scuttlebutt has it that Roger's wife Jessica is playing around (the rabbit bursts into floods of tears); and the next thing we know the silly creature has been framed for the murder of his producer's rival. After much disentanglement, it transpires that all the trouble has been caused by Judge Doom, who wants to take over Toontown and dunk its residents in a patented concoction known as 'The Dip', an acid bath for Toons, whose bumptiousness stems, it seems, partly from their former indestructibility.

The atmosphere of dog-eared Hollywood is nicely caught, as is the now discredited notion of the blow-torch effect of the old-fashioned vamp. In a nightclub, Eddie practically falls off his stool at the approach of the serpentine Jessica, while at his shoulder, in a beautiful touch, little Betty Boop looks on in wonder. Still, Jessica notwithstanding, the main attraction is Hoskins and the exasperating rabbit, and on the whole they do not disappoint. Roger is a creature fully formed: a chatterbox, a coward, a hopeless joker who will do anything for a laugh. He cannot hold his liquor, it literally blows the top of his head off – though on one occasion, like Popeye's spinach, it saves his life. But to reveal why would altogether spoil the fun.

Figure 26   Film review of *Who Framed Roger Rabbit* from *Sight and Sound*, Autumn 1988

She then picked out from the review the following words associated with this style of language and looked them up in *The Slang Thesaurus*.

Can you match them with their synonyms?

1 private eye	**a**	shabby
2 bad hats	**b**	to concoct false evidence against somebody
3 liquor	**c**	to flirt
4 scuttlebutt	**d**	disreputable people
5 dog-eared	**e**	alcohol
6 to play around	**f**	a detective
7 to frame somebody	**g**	a gossip

Type of film/genre
Cartoon: interaction of real with cartoon characters. Based on post-war Hollywood detective stories.

Setting
Hollywood 1947: Toontown, a ghetto where the Toons (the cartoon characters) live.

Main characters

Toons	*Humans*
Roger Rabbit	Eddie Valiant, a detective
Baby Herman	Judge Doom, a villain
Dwarfs	
3 Blue Birds	

Summary
Gossip has it that Roger's wife is playing around. Roger is falsely accused of murder. It transpires that the trouble has been caused by Judge Doom who wants to take over Toontown and dunk its residents in 'The Dip', an acid bath.

Language
American slang, typical of the type found in Hollywood detective movies associated with gangsters and crime.

Figure 27   English film assessment chart

Answers are on page 202.

Using the extracts from *The Slang Thesaurus* (see Figures 29 and 31), find out the meaning of 'dust' from *The Big Sleep*, and 'nab' from *The Dick Tracy Casebook*.

Can you think of other ways to prepare yourself before you see a film?

I moved towards the door. 'We'll trot along now,' I said, I took hold of her arm. She was staring at Eddie Mars. She liked him.

'Any message – if Geiger comes back,' Eddie Mars asked gently.

'We won't bother you.'

'That's too bad,' he said, with too much meaning. His grey eyes twinkled and then hardened as I went past him to open the door. He added in a casual tone: 'The girl can dust. I'd like to talk to you a little, soldier.'

I let go of her arm. I gave him a blank stare. 'Kidder, eh' he said nicely. 'Don't waste it. I've got two boys outside in a car that always do just what I want them to.'

Carmen made a sound at my side and bolted through the door. Her steps faded rapidly downhill. I hadn't seen her car, so she must have left it down below. I started to say: 'What the hell –!'

'Oh, skip it,' Eddie Mars sighed. 'There's something wrong around here. I'm going to find out what it is. If you want to pick lead out of your belly, get in my way.'

'Well, well,' I said, 'a tough guy.'

Figure 28 Extract from *The Big Sleep* by Raymond Chandler

MOTION: TRANSFERENCE

61. Transference

v. 1. *to transport, haul, carry:* cart, hump, pack, tote
2. *to pull:* schlep (Yid.), snake, yank
3. *to reach for:* make a long arm
4. *to raise:* hike

62. Throwing

n. 1. chuck, shy; spec. cricket use: dollydrop, skier, steepler
2. *hard throw:* bullet, hot one, hotshot, hummer, ripper, scorcher, sizzler, smoker, steamer, streaker, whizzer, zipper
v. 3. *to throw:* bung, chuck, cut loose (with), let go (of), rifle (it in), shy, smoke, uncork

63. Ejection

n. 1. *discharge, dismissal:* the air, the axe, big E, boot, boot-out, bounce, brush (off), bump, bum's rush, chuck, dust, elbow, gate, KB, kiss-off, knock-back, order of the boot, Spanish archer ('El Bow'), walking papers
v. 2. *to dismiss:* blow out, boot (out), bounce, bump, call it a day, chuck, ditch, eighty-six (rhy.sl. = nix), elbow, give the air, – the sack, the belt, – the brown envelope, – the (old) heave-ho, – the elbow, axe etc. (see n. 1), hoof out, put the skids under, – the screws to, sack, see the back off, send away with a flea in one's ear, send packing, show the door, – the gate, sling out, turf out; spec. kick upstairs (move to a senior but less important job)
3. *to be dismissed:* get the chop, – the bullet, – the order of the boot, – the sack, etc. (see n. 1.)

Figure 29 Extract 1 from *The Slang Thesaurus* by Jonathon Green

Figure 30   Extract from *The Dick Tracy Casebook*.
Copyright © by Tribune Media Services; reprinted by permission of Editors
Press Service, Inc.

POSSESSION: ACQUISITION
365. Acquisition; Gains
n. 1. goodies, killing, pickings,
rake-off, take
v. 2. *to obtain:* bag, collar, come in
for, cop, freeze onto, get one's
hooks on, glom, gobble up, land,
load up on, mop up, nab, nip, pull
down, rope in, rustle up, scare up,
snag, sneeze, whistle up; spec.
trouser (to pocket)
3. *to take everything:* go the whole
hog, sweep the board
4. *to obtain by fraud:* chisel out of,
ease out of, promote for, wangle out
of, work for (see also Influence: 219)
adv. 5. *gaining:* on a roll
phr. 6. *I want!:* bags I!, dibs on!

366. Possession; Property
n. 1. traps; spec. dead man's shoes
(property of a dead person); OPs
(other people's property)
2. *luggage:* bindle, keister
v. 3. *to have plenty:* be cochealed,
– lousy with, pack, reek with, roll
in, stink of, swim in
adj. 4. *supplied:* cochealed, stinking
adv. 5. *well-supplied:* crummy with,
filthy with, loaded, long on, lousy
with, rolling in, stinking with,
swimming in
6. *lacking:* clean out of, fresh out of
phr. 7. *how much do you have?:*
how are you fixed?; spec. are you
holding? (do you have drugs)

367. Joint Possession; Sharing
n. 1. piece, rake-off, shake, slice,
split; spec. Dutch treat (both parties
share payment); even Steven (fair
shares); short end, – straw (the
lesser share)
v. 2. *to share:* chip in, cut up, divvy
(up), go Dutch, – fifty-fifty,
– halves, – splits, muck in with,
split; spec. deck up (drug use)
3. *to give a share:* cut in, deal in,
give a cut, – a piece, etc. (see n. 1),
ring in, split with
4. *get one's share:* come in for, cut a
piece, – a slice, etc. (see n. 1), get a
cut, – a piece, – a slice, etc. (see n.
1); spec. get in the ground floor (get
a share at the outset); hog, muscle
into (take an extra share)
5. *to share out:* dish out
adv. 6. *sharing:* even Steven,
fifty-fifty, going halves, – Dutch
7. *excluded from a share:* out of the
game, – the picture, – the running

368. Borrowing and Begging
n. 1. *a request for something:* bite,
hit-up, mooch, shakedown, tap,
touch
v. 2. *to beg:* bite one's ear, bludge
(Aus.), bot (Aus.), brace
up, bum off, coat and badge
(rhy.sl. = cadge), fang (Aus.), get
into one's ribs, grub, make a touch,

Figure 31   Extract 2 from *The Slang Thesaurus* by Jonathon Green

Here are some suggestions:

- Listen as much as possible to recordings of different varieties of spoken English.

- If the film is based on a book, try to read this first. How true to the book was the film? Which did you prefer, the film or the book? Why?

Preparation like this also enabled Maria to find out about possible cultural references.

WHILE VIEWING

Although Maria's main reason for watching films in English was for pleasure, she made a point of noting down at least five new words or expressions during the film. She would find out their meanings after the film.

AFTER VIEWING

After the film, she often found it useful to read a review again and decide whether or not she agreed with it. She also kept a film diary in which she organized reviews and any preparation work; noted down vocabulary she wanted to learn; and made notes as to why or why not she would recommend a film.

Listening to native speakers

In her conversations with native speakers, we saw that Maria sometimes had problems understanding their replies. This was sometimes due to idiomatic expressions, unfamiliar accents, and specific cultural references. She decided that instead of nodding politely and giving the impression she had understood, she would ask people to explain what they meant when she didn't understand. She thought about ways she could do this and practised these phrases. For example,

● asking for repetition/ clarification/ explanation	*Can you say that again, please?* *I'm sorry?* *What does . . . mean, please?* *Could you explain what . . . means, please?*
● checking/confirming	Here the speaker repeats information using a rising intonation or uses expressions like: *Did you say . . .?* *Do you mean . . .?*
● reformulating	*Oh, you mean . . .* *Oh, like the . . .*

Here are some further suggestions for practising your listening.

● Listen to the radio as much as possible. Find out about frequencies and times of programmes of interest to you.

● Record talks you go to. Don't forget to ask the speaker's permission first.

● Cover up subtitles on your television at home when you watch films in English.

● Record the sound track of films or programmes you are interested in and build up a listening library. Exchange cassettes with a colleague.

● Borrow audio cassettes from a library.

ANSWERS (page 198)

1 f   2 d   3 e   4 g   5 a   6 c   7 b

Speaking

It can sometimes be difficult to find opportunities to practise speaking when you do not live in an English-speaking country. You may need to be quite ingenious to overcome this problem. Think about the possibilities you have for speaking English where you live.

In order to improve your speaking, you need to analyse which aspects to work on. One way of doing this is to record yourself. Look back at Chapter 8 at the section on learning the pronunciation of English which describes different pronunciation features. Use these as criteria to assess your recording. It is a good idea to focus on only one or two areas at a time. Also, look again at Chapter 13, Using storybooks, and use the self-assessment sheet to analyse other aspects of your spoken English. You may also like to record yourself describing a photograph or illustration. Always decide whether you are going to focus on your accuracy or your fluency or both.

ACTIVITY: BEING SPONTANEOUS!
To practise your fluency, respond to the following situations and record yourself. Do not prepare, respond immediately. Be spontaneous!

1 You have borrowed a friend's car but unfortunately have just scraped the right wing getting out of a tight parking place. You know your friend will be furious. What will you say?

2 You have just been shopping and realize you have left your purse/wallet in the cheese shop. You go back immediately but they have just closed. You can see an assistant who is still in the shop but just getting ready to leave.

3 You are in a well-known restaurant. The rare steak you ordered is medium. You want to change it.

4 Your neighbour is playing their record player so loudly that you can't even hear the television in your own flat. You knock on their door to complain.

Now listen to your recording. What did you do well? What did you not do so well? Why? Are there any changes you would like to make? On page 204, you will find suggested responses to the above situations. How do they compare with yours?

Try to think of possible situations where you may need to speak English, and practise in the same way as above.

Starting a conversation

When you are in an English-speaking country, do you often want to start a conversation with someone, for example, at a bus stop, on a bus, in a train, in a café, but are not sure what to say? Here are some suggestions to get a conversation going.

1 Make a statement or ask a question which is very general. In Britain, people often talk about the weather. However, if you make an obvious statement, for example, *It's cold!*, the other person may only agree with you and make no effort to contribute anything further. Try adding a question, *It's cold for June. Is it usually as cold as this in June?*

2 Begin with a compliment. For example, *That's a very beautiful building. Do you know when it was built?* or *I love London. What's it like living here?* The questions invite the other person to give information or a personal opinion.

3 Babies and dogs provide an ideal pretext to start a conversation. *What a beautiful baby! Is it a boy or a girl? How old is she?* and so on; or *A chow! We used to have a chow. How old is he? Is he friendly?*

4 Establish your social identity as a foreigner. People are often proud to tell you about their country and places to visit in the vicinity. *I'm from . . . and on holiday here. Could you tell me if there are any interesting places to visit in your town?*

Can you think of any other ways of starting a conversation?

Here are some further suggestions for practising your spoken English.

- Learn set phrases and practise them regularly.

- Instead of writing to your correspondent, send a cassette letter.

- Join a club where you can meet other people and have conversations in English.

- Practise reading stories and rhymes aloud and record yourself.

- Have imaginary conversations.

- Rehearse language you will need in the classroom, such as language for playing games, for giving instructions, social chit chat and so on. See Chapter 17 for further details.

- Set up a Language Clinic. See Chapter 11, Classroom management, for details.

SUGGESTED REPLIES FOR PAGES 202–3

1 I really am sorry to tell you this but while the car was parked in Albert Street someone scraped the right wing. They didn't even leave a note! I do hope your insurance will cover the repairs. Drivers in London are awful, aren't they?

2 (Knocking loudly on the shop window and beckoning to the shop assistant) Hey! Hey! Excuse me! Can you open the door, please? Please! Thank you. I'm sorry to bother you but I think I've left my wallet in the shop. Have you found one? Could I please come in and look?

3 Waiter! I ordered a rare steak and this one is medium! I'd like another one that's rare.

4 Excuse me. Would you please turn your record player down because it's so loud I can't even hear myself think in my own flat!

Reading

You may find that much of the reading you do in English is for your job, such as articles, handbooks, reports, and so on. Try to find some time, however, for reading for pleasure. Reading a variety of different text types, such as novels, plays, magazine articles, advertisements, and so on will give you plenty of exposure to authentic English and will help you improve other skills too.

When reading for your job, you will want to read quickly, selectively and accurately.

There is an enormous number of books and articles about

English language teaching to choose from. Here is an approach you could try which will help you select the reading materials you need.

Selecting and rejecting

- Read reviews and catalogue descriptions about publications. These can give you an idea about current trends and often provide a useful summary.

- If possible, get hold of annotated bibliographies which give you a brief description of what a book or an article is about.

- Make sure the book or article is not too difficult for you. If the first page has more than five words you do not understand, look for another one.

- If you are interested in finding out about current approaches to language teaching, check the date of publication.

- Is there a summary at the beginning or end of an article, or at the end of each chapter, or a conclusion at the end of the book? These can save you time. If there is no summary, then read the first and last paragraph to help you decide if it will be useful for you.

Reading quickly

When reading, the eyes move in a series of stops and quick jumps. Good readers can read up to five words without moving their eyes because they can skip and guess as they are familiar with certain combinations of words. People who read one word at a time and who skip back over words and letters are very slow readers and will not be able to understand much of what they read. They usually do this because they are anxious about not understanding every word. Slower readers also have to work harder than faster readers because they have to add the meaning of each word to the meaning of each following word. This may result in boredom and loss of concentration, and they may lose the meaning of what they are reading. Try to read in chunks to speed up your reading. Your eyes will be doing less physical work and the rhythm and flow of your reading will carry you through the meaning.

Reading strategies

Good readers understand their purpose for reading and vary their reading strategy accordingly. Do you agree with the explanations of the following four strategies?

Strategy	Description	Purpose
Detailed reading	reading very carefully	complete under-standing
Reading for pleasure	reading at whatever speed suits you	enjoyment
Skimming	looking at a text quickly to find out what it's about	general idea
Scanning	reading for specific information	finding details

Figure 32   Reading strategies

ACTIVITY: READING A NEWSPAPER ARTICLE

1 Look at the title and sub-title of the article in Figure 33. Decide on your purpose for reading it and select the appropriate strategy.
2 List the points for and against the pilot scheme in a chart like the one below. What reading strategy did you use to complete this activity?

For	Against

Here are some further ideas for practising your reading.

● Join a library where you can borrow books in English.

● Take out a subscription to an English language teaching maga-zine or journal or newspaper. See the Appendix for further de-tails.

● Collect articles on subjects of particular interest to you.

● Ask to be put on publishers' mailing lists so you are sent their catalogues and details about new publications and presentations and talks given by authors. You can usually get a list of publishers represented in your country, and their addresses, by writing to the British Council.

Getting a young tongue round the achtung

Another attempt to teach foreign languages in primary schools is taking place, this time in Scotland. Kay Smith reports

PUPILS at Ferguslie primary in Paisley, near Glasgow, are getting their first taste of a foreign language as one of 52 primaries taking part in a pilot scheme run by Strathclyde regional council.

Situated in one of Scotland's most severely deprived areas, the school – its windows covered with metal grids – looks as if it has been designed to withstand raids from warring neighbourhood tribes. But inside its 10- and 11-year-olds are looking to Europe.

Every week they are taught German for two 30-minute sessions by Sheila Hart, a teacher from a nearby secondary school. She encourages them to engage in simple social chat about their families, hobbies and that perennial British topic, the weather.

Class teachers sit in on Hart's lessons, picking up the language themselves and helping with group activities. When the secondary specialist leaves, the primary teacher can create further opportunities for pupils to practice their new language.

Teacher Gail Copeland has reverted to the methods of the infant classroom. A Wendy House, a café, and a shop full of plastic hamburgers and German comics give opportunities for role playing. Meanwhile colleague David Scott has taught graph work based on a survey of the children's hobbies, a good excuse for a bold wall chart using German words.

Critics of the pilot scheme say a foreign language is irrelevant to young Scots who travel abroad far less frequently than their European counterparts. But Copeland points out that the German-Swiss drugs company CIBA Geigy is a major employer in Paisley, and that the events in Germany and Eastern Europe are constantly on the children's television sets. "German is easy, in any case, for west-coasters to pick up because of our accents."

French or German is being taught in each of the pilots but the implications of children with skills in either of these languages turning up in secondaries has not yet been thought through. Head Ian Fraser, though, is pleased with the exercise in improving liaison with the secondary school.

The response from parents has been positive, he says. "They see German as enhancing their children's education."

Strathclyde has adopted its pilots ahead of other Scottish regions. Last year it put up £500,000 to mount trial schemes in six secondary schools and their 36 feeder primaries. Now it is extending its pilots to another 26 secondaries and 146 primaries. Earlier age classes will be involved, with Spanish and Italian being taught as well as French and German, and £420,000 has been allocated for extra staff to release secondary teachers into the primaries.

Despite the caution urged by the Educational Institute of Scotland, the country's biggest teachers' union, the only negative parental reaction has been from those who think their child is not getting enough French or German.

Strathclyde modern languages adviser Sandy Wilson brushes aside EIS warnings of a repetition of the "botched up" experiments which crept up from England in the sixties: "The aim is to investigate the desirability of teaching modern languages at this stage."

Figure 33   Extract from *Education Guardian*, 29 May 1990

Writing

Many people who speak English fluently and effectively often feel anxious at having to write in English.

How do you feel about writing? Complete the following questionnaire for your own language and for English to help you focus on your attitudes. Put a (√) for Yes and a (×) for No.

	Your language	English
1 Do you feel confident about writing whenever you have to?		
2 Can you write in different styles, e.g., personal and formal letters, reports, narrative?		
3 If you need help with your writing, are there people you can ask?		
4 Are you clear about your purpose when you write?		
5 Do you write drafts and then edit them?		
6 Do you try to avoid having to write if possible?		
7 Do you enjoy writing?		
8 Do you ever write just for yourself?		
9 Is your handwriting fairly readable and quick?		

Product or process?

Recently, there has been a shift of focus in the teaching and learning of writing from analysing the features of finished texts to a process approach to writing. This approach looks at what good writers actually do as they write, which includes processes like noting down ideas at random, organizing them, writing drafts and editing.

Here are some of these processes.

GETTING STARTED

Getting started can often be the most difficult part of writing. Most writers start by making notes. These may be no more than a list of words or points. A list like this can help in two ways. First, it acts as a reminder. We often get so carried away with one particular aspect of a subject or a point we want to make that we sometimes forget to mention other points that are equally important. Second, notes can help establish how you are going to organize your ideas and provide a structure for your piece of writing.

DRAFTING

Once you have made some notes, you can write your first draft. Don't worry about finding the right words or correct spelling at this stage. Concentrate more on what you want to say.

EDITING

When you have written your first draft, the editing process can begin. Here are four areas to look for when you edit.

1 Editing for meaning. Does your draft make sense?
  - It often helps to read your draft aloud. This can highlight parts which are unclear.
  - If you have time, leave it for a while and come back to it when your original ideas aren't so fresh in your mind.
  - Leave lots of room, if you write a second draft, for crossing out and adding in.

2 Editing for grammar. Here you are checking and changing so that words and phrases are put together in the best way for your purpose. This also includes editing for punctuation, which helps the writer communicate.

3 Editing for spelling.
  - Underline or circle the words that look wrong and continue reading.
  - Use a good dictionary to check spelling.

4 Editing for presentation. This involves the overall layout.
  - What kind of presentation would best communicate your message to your reader(s)?
  - Do you have access to a typewriter or word processor?

TASK: Describing a teaching experience

Read and compare the following extracts. The first comes from a letter written by a teacher of English in Brazil and, the second, from an article in the *English Language Teaching Journal* which describes a teaching project in Indonesia. What language do the writers use to describe their experiments? How does this affect the style?

The letter

> The group consists of eighteen 9–10 year-olds who have up to this month covered 130 hours of English using Heinemann's SNAP! (stages 1 and 2). We meet twice a week for a 75 minute-lesson. What I have been doing since March is the following: after each lesson (or at least once a week) I ask them to tell each other what they considered to have been the 'main teaching point' of the class event. They usually come up with different ideas (either focussing on lexis, grammar, functions or skills) and this helps me prepare the following lesson-plans or even remedial sessions.
>
> Also, I have started (still based on the same idea) to ask them to help me isolate during the lesson (after presentation and before the practice stage block) what language (either grammar or function) they recognize as *new*. This gives them a share of the responsibility for 'planning' the lesson along with me as well as developing their awareness of the purpose of input blocks printed in the materials and teaching/learning aims for the event.
>
> Still, in the area of organizing new lexical items, the experience has proved very successful. After each lesson students are asked to write in their copybooks three new words (preferably nouns) to be illustrated at home in their *My Picture Dictionary*. They look up the new item and in case they find a picture, they colour it and write its name underneath. If the picture is not there they draw or cut and glue a picture, colour it and write its name. Every second week I ask pairs of students to go through their dictionaries showing each other what they have done – I can then select one letter of the alphabet, or a specific vocabulary set (such as furniture items, animals etc.) – and ask them to add new words, correct spelling etc.

The article

Total Physical Response

In most provinces the students in Class 1 of the junior high schools who are taught by PKG* teachers spend the first five or six weeks of their English course (five 45-minute lessons per week) responding to instructions in English from their teacher. The responses are mainly physical and involve individual, small group, and whole class reactions to contextualized instructions – for example, Teacher: 'Who lives on Jalan Heng Lekir? Stand up if you live on Jalan Heng Lekir. Henny, take four flowers from the vase on my table. Give a flower to each student who lives on Jalan Heng Lekir'. Some of the responses also involve drawing or simple writing, and some involve group reading in English and group discussion in Indonesian.

Using TPR, the teachers are able to introduce most of the vocabulary and structures in the curriculum for Semester 1 in a way which interests and involves the students and does not judge or threaten them at all. In this way, teachers are also able to introduce many of the communicatively significant structures, such as relative clauses and the first conditional, which are usually saved until later in the course because of their formal complexity. For example, 'Give the flowers to the girl who is wearing a red watch. If I cry, touch the shoulder of the person next to you.'

* PKG = Permantapan Kerja Guru: Strengthening of the work of Teacher's Project.

'Managing change in Indonesian high schools': Brian Tomlinson *ELTJ*, Vol. 44/1, 25–37.

Now write a letter or a short article describing a teaching experience you have been involved in. Remember to convey the information clearly providing background information about your learners and the context, details of the experience and its rationale, and some kind of evaluation. Refer back to the guide-lines above for drafting and editing.

Here are some further suggestions for practising writing:

- Prepare some worksheets for your pupils. See Chapter 10 for further details.

- Keep a teaching diary or a personal diary in English.

- Write letters to a correspondent in English.

- Learn to type or use a word processor and copy different text types, for example, recipes, rhymes, stories, riddles, letters and so on.

- Cut out and keep examples of different types of written English, for example, letters, reports, advertisements, worksheets and so on, which you can use for reference.

- Write a story for your pupils.

- Create a teacher's newsletter. Get together with other colleagues and publish a newsletter for other teachers in your area.

- Write to your pupils. Write notes or riddles to your pupils from time to time and invite them to reply. For example, 'It's black and white, it's got wings but it can't fly, it lives in the Antarctic. What is it?'

References and further reading

Allsop, J., 1990. *Test Your Phrasal verbs:* Penguin English.

Davies, E. and N. Whitney, 1984. *Study Skills for Reading*: Heinemann.

Ellis, G. and B. Sinclair, 1989. *Learning to Learn English*: Cambridge University Press.

Hedge, T., 1988. *Writing*: Oxford University Press.

Sheerin, S., 1989. *Self-Access*: Oxford University Press.

Soars, J. and L., 1989. *Headway Advanced*: Oxford University Press.

Watcyn-Jones, P., 1990. *Test Your English Idioms*: Penguin English.

17 *English in the classroom*

For many years now, teaching a foreign language has not been a question of teaching pupils about the language (even if, as has already been discussed, the teaching given includes phases of reflecting on the language). Rather, it has been about teaching in the language, from the very first beginners' lesson onwards. Primary school English teachers are no exception to this rule, no matter whether English is a second language for them, as for their pupils, or whether they are English native speakers.

There is, in the first place, a psychological reason for this change. Students, whether children or adults, need to feel from the start that they are not learning another living language just to add a further field of knowledge and an extra academic subject to their studies. They primarily set out to be proficient in the use of an alternative means of communication, in order to be able to take part in linguistic exchanges with people who speak the language. This is a very powerful initial motivation and is founded, as a matter of principle, on the presupposition that anything can be said in this other language, not just what is to be found within the confines of more or less artificial formal exercises.

The pedagogical reason for the change is clear. As English, by definition, is the language of the English class, then the opportunities to learn English, and to hear and speak it, are considerably increased when teachers in particular are careful to ensure the communicative (the specialist term is 'pragmatic') authenticity of the exchanges they find themselves supervising.

One of the major objectives, therefore, of teachers who are not English native speakers is to become truly proficient in the English of oral communication, which corresponds to the main functions required for classroom situations and to basic notions (identity, nature, dimension, colour, quantity, possession, place, etc.). These functions and notions are expressed in English, as in other languages, by what are known as 'speech acts', a term which clearly indicates that, in verbal exchanges between people, it is always a question of an **action** which is usually aimed at obtaining a **reaction** from the listener.

For ease of reference, the following two sets of examples are classified by function of communication and by classroom activity.

The main functions of communication in English

RESPECTING SOCIAL CONVENTIONS

● Greeting people
  Good morning, (or *Good afternoon,*) children, teacher, (Mr, Miss, Mrs) *Dupont* . . .
  (less formal) *Hello, . . .,* or *Hi, . . .* /hai/, an American form which is in general use amongst young British people

● Introducing oneself
  I'm (Peter Heywood, Jean Leblanc, . . .), your (the) English teacher.

● Introducing somebody else
  This is Mary and this is Juliet.
  Hello, Mary. Hello, Juliet. (or *Nice to meet you.*)

● Asking about somebody's health
  How are you (today)?
  I'm very well (or *I'm fine*), *thank you.*
  And how are you? (*You* is stressed.)
  I'm very well too.

● Giving and thanking
  This is (a present) for you.
  Thank you (so/very much).

● Apologizing
  I'm sorry (for being late), . . .
  I apologize . . .
  (when inconveniencing somebody) *Excuse me, (please).*

GIVING AND RECEIVING INFORMATION
NB As there are no clear divisions between functions, some of the examples given above also fall into this category.

● Identity
  Are you Henry Steward? No, I'm his brother.

● Profession
  Is he a musician? Yes, and he's an actor.

● Nature of an object
  'What is it? (It's) a box.
  Is it a dog or a cat?

● Dimension, height, distance
  How big is your bag? It's not very big.

How tall is that famous basketball player?/About six feet.
How far is the school?/Only three hundred yards.

● Colour
What colour is your book?/(It's) blue and yellow.

● Possession
Whose pen is this?/(I think) it's Jane's.

● Quantity
How many boys are there?
Only five, but there are twenty girls.

● Reason and cause:
Why are you late?/Because my mother is ill.

GETTING THE LISTENER TO DO SOMETHING
This is usually at the teacher's request, which is reflected by the list below, but the pupils may also be the initiators in game situations and in a great many other activities.

● Using a command, an injunction, an instruction
Stand up, Come here, Go to the board, Go back to your seat, Sit down.
Look (here), Look at the picture (the board, your books, page 16, . . .).
Listen (carefully), Listen to me (John, Susan, Myriam, the song, . . .).
Repeat after me (after Richard, . . .).
Ask Joan (Robert, Tom, Betty, your neighbour).
Ask me (him, her, . . .) a question.
Answer her (his, my) question.
Spell your name (the word, . . .).

● Using a polite request or an invitation
Lend me your book, please.
Help me, will you?
Can you show me your picture?
Please raise your hands.

NB Generally speaking, polite forms of expression are used more frequently in English than in other languages. Sometimes they are even used as a way of camouflaging an imperative accompanied by a degree of impatience:
Now, will you please keep quiet!

● Making a suggestion
How about a little game now?
What about learning a new song?

EXPRESSING AN OPINION, A JUDGEMENT, A PREFERENCE

Learning to speak a foreign language involves learning to be able to express tastes, preferences and aversions with the same degree of freedom as in the mother tongue. Young children are very ready to try this given the chance.

- About different sports
  Do you like football (soccer)?
  Yes, I do. I love it. or *No, I hate it; it's very boring.*

  Which sport do you like best? Tennis is my favourite.
  I prefer basketball.

- About pastimes and holidays
  What do you do on Sundays?
  I like watching television. or
  I like playing with my brothers and sisters. or
  I prefer cycling or swimming.

- About different singers, actors, books, films
  I like Jean-Paul Belmondo: he's very funny.
  I think he's silly.

  Look at this picture. Do you like it?
  Oh, yes. It's a lovely picture.
  I don't like it at all.

English for various classroom occasions and activities

WARMING UP AT THE START OF A LESSON

Hello, children (boys and girls).
Good morning, teacher (Mr X, Miss Y, Mrs Z).

How are you?
Fine, thank you. Not too bad.

What's the matter with you, Tim?
I'm tired.
You went to bed too late!

Look at the sky. What's the weather like?
Lovely. Cloudy. It's going to rain.

It goes without saying that the pupils are not in a position to invent anything for themselves. It is through hearing comments like the above every lesson, and taking part when they feel ready to do so, that they will gradually assimilate the phrases and acquire confidence in their use.

REVIEWING THE PREVIOUS LESSON

Care should be taken to use a strictly limited number of ways of speaking about the past with pupils who are beginners, up until the time when they have been taught and have assimilated the forms of the simple past tense using *did* and the irregular forms of some of the common verbs. Taking the class register can provide a useful means of making the transition if the teacher makes sure, through the use of gestures and a few of the pupils' names, that the question which quickly becomes a ritual is properly understood from the start: *Is everybody here today? No, Sandra is not here. Thank you, Bob. Everybody is here except Sandra.*

Now, listen everybody. Do you remember the last lesson? What do you remember? The bad boy and the nice dog. Yes, the bad boy lost his bag and the dog . . .

The pupils can then be encouraged to recapitulate the main points of the short picture story by the teacher, who will also ensure that the various key words are repeated and understood by means of gestures, miming and the use of appropriate illustrations.

THE CONTENT OF THE DAY'S LESSON

Listen to me, please. The new lesson is about Betty going to the zoo with her parents. We're going to learn the names of six animals at the zoo. Do you know what a zoo is?

Betty will ask questions about these animals. She will learn a lot of interesting things. And we will learn with her. Then we will learn a new song. All right?

What a pity Sandra is not here today! We will tell her about Betty at the zoo tomorrow.

STARTING OFF AN ACTIVITY

Useful phrases: commands and requests for information

Listen everybody. Are you all ready? Then we can start.
Look at this picture.
Listen to the tape.
Say this word (sentence) with me.
Open your books at page eight.
Look at the pictures and listen again.
Take your copybooks and your pens or pencils.
Draw an elephant and a giraffe.
Write the words 'elephant' and 'giraffe' under the pictures.
Now shut your books and copybook.
We're going to talk about . . .

INDIVIDUAL HELP DURING AN ACTIVITY
Is everything all right?
Now, Tim, ask Harry where the cat is.
Harry, can you answer the question?, Who can?
Good! But be careful; is she on the basket or in the basket?
What's this?, Are you sure?
Say it again. Write the name again.
What are you drawing?, Look at page eight again.
Look at the board everyone.
Read the sentence, Bill, Susan, Bob, . . .
Take your copybooks and write it down.

ENDING AN ACTIVITY
Have you all finished?
Stop drawing (writing).
Is everything clear?, Any questions?
Remember the new words (and their pronunciation!)
Now we're going to learn a little poem.

CORRECTING MISTAKES (after encouragement)
Any active effort made by a pupil to participate should be encouraged
(*Yes, Janet, good!, Right! Good for you., Well done!*) and this encouragement makes it easier for the pupil to accept any correction
which may be necessary: *Good, but you can say it better. Will you
repeat?/I haven't finish./No. Listen. Betty, will you say it for her?/I
haven't finished./Yes, that's it. Susan, can you say it now?*

Such help from their peers is readily accepted, provided the
pupils making the mistakes or omissions are themselves given the
opportunity to correct the word, sound, or major point of grammar,
so that they too manage to do as well as their friends.

Clearly, not too much time should be spent on correction and it
may be preferable to group the corrections together into a brief
session of self-evaluation and self-correction or '*co-correction*',
conducted with the aid of the teacher at the end of the lesson.

ENDING A LESSON
Well, that's enough for today., It's time to finish,
Time is up.
You've been very good.
Have you all finished?
Shut your books: it's time to clear up.
Hurry up!
Remember what we learned today . . .
For your homework, you'll have to read the little poem again . . .

Myriam, will you please collect the drawings with the new words.
When is our next lesson?
I will tell you a new story, a very nice story.
Goodbye, everyone. See you next Friday.

Which metalanguage to use?

According to the great linguist, Roman Jakobson, one of the six
basic functions of language is 'metalinguistic'. The purpose of this
function is to make it possible to analyse the code which is used, if
only to be able to make better use of it. Everybody uses the
metalinguistic function at times, when asking themselves about
the form or meaning of some element in their mother tongue.
French people, for instance, do not usually know the meaning of
the French word '*palifier*'. However, their dictionaries will tell them
that it is a transitive verb, conjugated like '*fortifier*' (to fortify),
which comes from the noun '*pal*' (stake) and means '*fortifier un
terrain a l'aide de pals ou de pilotis*' (to fortify a piece of ground using
stakes or piles). In providing this description, the dictionary uses a
metalanguage made up partly of words from everyday language
(or technical language) which have been taken out of context and
placed between inverted commas, and partly from a certain
amount of terminology (verb, transitive, noun, etc.).

Nowadays, it is accepted that infants, who start acquiring language from birth onwards (partly through contact with the language of their families and others around them and partly thanks
to a natural human faculty), already have an unconscious appreciation of metalanguage. Clearly, they do not ask themselves about
the function of this language but the mere fact that they very
quickly know how to attract attention using appropriate noises
and how to make it understood that they are hungry, thirsty or
want to move, indicates that the essential phenomena of linguistic
interaction are being developed. Studies of language development
in children have highlighted the early appearance of a true 'two-
word phrase' (using a form of baby-talk, naturally) in which the
order of the 'words' is respected.

In English classes at primary school, it is usually possible to
count on the presence of this 'unconscious metalinguistic activity',
which has been developed in the mother tongue. However, there
are two reasons for suggesting it is beneficial if this 'activity' is
encouraged to happen consciously through short periods of reflection:

1 The children are accustomed to this happening at school where

they are encouraged to consolidate and develop what they have acquired naturally in other areas through the teaching they receive.

2 As there will be differences between the way English and their mother tongue function, it is helpful for them to be aware of the differences (and, indeed, the similarities). This has the double advantage of making it easier to learn the foreign language and of increasing their proficiency in their mother tongue.

Starting this process at the beginning of their first year will obviously mean working in the mother tongue. However, it will quite rapidly become evident to the teacher that the basic terminology needed can equally well be given in English, without posing any particularly insurmountable problems of comprehension. In this way, the pupils will gradually learn to use these parts of the metalanguage for themselves.

A guide to the English terms which most closely approximate to those in French and which might be of use is given in the following list. The advice of Eric Hawkins, a teacher, should not, however, be overlooked. He recommends that the pupils should first of all have a concept of the functions of the various parts of speech before trying to name them. Unless they have already learnt the equivalent French terminology, it is better, at first, to leave the children to invent their own names before inflicting the official terminology on them (Hawkins, 1984).

SPOKEN ENGLISH (PRONUNCIATION)
sounds (rather than the technical term *phonemes*), *vowels* (*long, short*)
diphthongs, consonants, stress, stressed, unstressed
syllables (*first, second, . . ., last*)
rhythm (breathing intervals)
intonation (*going up, down*)

VOCABULARY
content words (= lexical items)
nouns, adjectives [ædʒɪktɪvz], *adverbs, verbs*

GRAMMAR
Grammatical words (‡content words)
auxiliary verbs (be, have, will, do)
modals (can, may, should)
articles [a, an, ʻthe, θ (= no article)]
possessives [pəˈzesɪvz] (my, your, . . .)

demonstratives (this, that, . . .)
nouns
pronouns (I, he, she, . . .)
prepositions (at, in, to, . . .)
conjunctions (and, but, or, . . .)
relatives (who, which, . . .)
sentence
subject, object

Grammatical endings
plural (‡ *singular*) (boys[z]; cats[s]; watches[ɪz])
tenses [ɪz]:
– *simple present* (*third person*); he runs[z], speaks[s], watches [ɪz].
– *present continuous* (he's singing)
– *simple past*: he arrived[d], looked[t], added [ɪd]
– *past participle*: he's punished
comparative: taller
superlative: the tallest [ɪst]

Ensuring the authenticity of the English Learnt

This chapter on English in the classroom would not be complete without a plea for the authenticity both of the English offered as a model and of the English accepted in the exchanges which are an essential part of foreign language classes. It would, perhaps, be best to state once again what this implies. For a long time now, the pedagogy of language teaching has placed great importance on using real texts and documents in the classroom, rather than the sorts of texts which are expressly drawn up or recorded for pedagogical purposes, albeit in the foreign language. In terms of the quality of pronunciation, the notion of authenticity refers to the quality of the phonological system, the rhythm, and the intonation, which should all be as close as possible to the standards of a native speaker, without seeking perfection, as this would make it impossible for non-native speakers to become foreign language teachers – not something to be encouraged. It does, on the other hand, mean that what is known as 'classroom English' is unacceptable. This variety of English, only heard inside the walls of French classrooms (and those of other non-English speaking countries), can cause problems of comprehension even for native speakers in extreme cases 'exaggeratedly slow delivery, resulting in inaccurate rhythm and intonation; displacement or disappearance of stress on words and sentences; seriously deformed sounds; etc.). What then is the best course of action?

Choice of texts and documents

- Keep to texts drawn up (and, where appropriate, recorded) by, or in close collaboration with, native speakers.

- Collect examples of texts published for English native speakers such as newspaper articles, books, magazines, catalogues and all kinds of brochures. These can serve as models of written English.

- Do the same thing for aural and audio-visual material (records, cassettes, cartoons, songs, poems, stories, games).

- Choose a coursebook and complementary material which guarantee completely the authenticity of the language used.

The teacher's English

A great deal of guidance has already been given in this chapter on the demands which teachers should make concerning the English of both their pupils and themselves. The two preceding chapters provided information on the best way for teachers to evaluate themselves and improve their proficiency in English.

The quality of the English spoken by teachers (and consequently, if indirectly, their pupils) obviously involves all the components of language: grammar, vocabulary, phonology and, indeed, what may be referred to as 'ability to communicate'.

Whatever their training, teachers who are not English native speakers should be constantly seeking to improve their English by establishing contacts with English speakers, by listening frequently to English language radio broadcasts, records and cassettes, and by watching English language films, videos and television broadcasts. Preparation of lessons should include preliminary practice of what is to be said in class, including what the pupils will be asked to say. Teachers should also check their knowledge of the different language components which will be relevant to the lesson by reference to the coursebook, the teacher's book, and various works of reference, such as:

- a good English grammar book

- a good monolingual dictionary and a good bilingual dictionary

- a good dictionary of pronunciation (a recent edition of the well-known *English Pronouncing Dictionary* by Daniel Jones, as revised by A. C. Gimson using his improved version of the international phonetic alphabet, should be a frequently consulted part of the library of every English teacher)

- in the case of English for communication, it is worthwhile consulting not just the English curriculum for primary schools (from the particular Ministry of Education) but also, as works of reference, *Waystage*, by J. van Ek and J. Trim (1991) and *A Communicative Grammar of English*, by G. Leech and J. Svartvik (1975)

Taking care to ensure 'authenticity of communication' means saying and having the pupils say what would be said by native speakers in similar situations, for the purposes of greeting each other, asking questions, expressing astonishment, offering congratulations, excusing themselves, etc. At the same time, care needs to be exercised to ensure the plausibility and relevance of what is said. Questions like *Are cats green?*, which cropped up frequently in earlier coursebooks, are good examples of false communication, unless the question is being addressed to a child who has coloured a drawing of a cat green for fun, or out of an unusual artistic bent. Such care should not however be extended to a different sort of false communication (or pseudo-communication according to Wilga Rivers) where teachers, for pedagogical and learning purposes, ask questions which are relevant but to which they already know the answers (*Is the boy in the picture pleased?*, *Where is she going?*, etc.). Nevertheless, this should not be overdone and teachers will be well-advised to put their minds to creating situations (through roleplay, for example) which give rise to real, and therefore authentic, questions and replies.

The reason why pronunciation occupies a position of particular importance in English teaching with reference to the other language components is well known. It is often considered, with reason, to be the biggest stumbling block for French native speakers because the two phonologies are completely different. That this is the case, is demonstrated, once again, in the following paragraph.

The English used in classroom exchanges

Naturally, this is specified in terms of the same components. Exchanges are not considered acceptable unless they satisfy a 'communication need', according to the definition of language put forward by A. Martinet (Martinet, 1960). The role of the teacher may be readily compared to that of the parents of young children in the natural acquisition process (*'Papa pati'* – *'Oui, papa est parti'*) ('Yes, daddy's gone') or, depending on the circumstances, *'papa va partir'* ('daddy's going'). Teachers have to be careful not to allow exchanges containing inaccurate utterances to go uncorrected, otherwise such utterances may be wrongly assumed to be perfectly admissible, given the teacher's (approving?) silence. However, any

correction made by the teacher or another pupil need not involve
the whole class. It can be gone over with the pupil who made the
mistake whenever the teacher considers best, as was the case in
the example given earlier concerning the use of the root of the
verb *finish* instead of the past participle *finished*. This indicated,
perhaps, that the pupil in question was experiencing problems
pronouncing the last consonant which, in turn, was creating
uncertainty about the grammar. Repeated interventions are therefore to be avoided, as they are paralysing. Instead, great vigilance
should be combined with taking the pupils back frequently to the
definitive model offered by the teacher, the tape or the book.

Teachers will find it that much easier to exercise greater vigilance concerning the phonological quality of the English spoken by
their pupils if they themselves are more aware of the difficulties.

Some traps in the pronunciation of English

Vowels

● Vowel sounds in English, and in the majority of other languages,
are not the same as in French. This is true even for those which
seem most similar. The [ɪ] in *sit* is not as closed as the vowel in
the French word *'dites'*, the [e] in *bed* is between the vowels in
'été' and in *'bête'*.

● All vowels (as opposed to diphthongs) in English are distin-
guished by being short (lax) or long (tense). The following
'minimal pairs' owe their difference to this fact:

short	long
sin[ɪ]	seem[ɪː]
full[ʊ]	fool[uː]
pot[ɒ]	port[ɔː]

Similarly differentiated are:
cupboard /ə/   bird[ɜː]
cat /æ/   cart[ɑː]

● The two vowels [e] and [ʌ] are short and have no long equiva-
lents.

● English may not have any nasal vowels (like the four in
French, as in the words *'pan'*, *'pont'*, *'pain'* and *'brun'*), but
it does have eight diphthongs where there are none in French.
This explains the difficulty French native speakers have in
making a distinction aurally between long vowels and diphthongs,
and in pronouncing them correctly:

with a long vowel	with a diphthong
bought[ɔː]	boat[əʊ]
law[ɔː]	low[əʊ]
pour[ɔː]	poor[ʊə]

Consonants

- The situation is basically the same as for the vowels; nearly all the English consonants are different from those in non-Germanic languages. The exceptions are some of the fricatives which are nearly identical ([f], [v], [s], [z], [ʃ], [ʒ]) and the two nasals [m] and [n].

- The English plosives [p] and [b] are bilabial but the voiceless [p] at the beginning of a word is stronger in English, involving a slight 'explosion'. This is evident in the difference between the French *'parc'* and the English *park* or the French *'pot'* and the English *pot*.

- The dentals [t] and [d] (tongue against teeth) in French and other languages correspond to the 'alveolars' in English (tip of the tongue slightly above the upper teeth). This can be appreciated by contrasting the French word *'tape'* with the English word *tap*.

- The English consonants [k] and [g] are produced with the back of the tongue (dorsum) against the velum, but placed further back than in French. The voiceless [k] has the same characteristic as [p] (slight 'explosion' at the beginning of a word). A comparison of the French *'cas'* with the English *cat* will show this.

- English has two consonants which are liquids [l] and [r] but with particular characteristics:
  - [1] has the same sound as in French at the beginning of a word (cf. *light* and *'lumiere'*). However, at the end of a word (*feel*) and when followed by a final consonant it becomes dark, as if combined with the vowel [u] in *book*.
  - the English [r] is very different to the guttural French consonant which, in any case, is transcribed differently ([R]). It is quite close to the French [L] but with an additional faint vibration. This can be seen by pronouncing the French adverb *'très'* with a strong English accent (between *'tché'* and *'tlé'*) and then saying the English words *red*, *road*, *right* (quite like *light*).

- There are an additional six consonants in English, which are not present in French and which often cause difficulties:
  - the two affricates [ts], pronounced tch, as in *child* or *Charles*, and [dʒ] as in *jeans, John, George,* etc.
  - the nasal consonant [ŋ] of *-ng* endings as in *song, bring,* etc., pronounced with the back of the tongue against the velum, as for [k] and [ᵬ], but with the difference that air is allowed to escape via the nose during the period of occlusion in the mouth, as for [m] and [n]. In order to pronounce the word *sing* correctly, care needs to be taken to avoid the pronunciations used in the following French words:

    'signe' (there is no English equivalent to the French consonant [ñ])

    'sain' [sɛ̃]. (there are no nasal vowels in English)

    'sain' followed by the consonant [ᵬ]. (the introduction of this [ᵬ] in words such as *singer, singing,* and *bringing* is to be avoided at all costs)
  - the pair of fricatives, [θ] as in *thick* and [ð] as in *this,* are two consonants (voiceless and voiced) for the single spelling 'th'. In order to avoid confusion with the two fricatives [s]–[z] (Mme Satcher; ze Prime Minister), the two fricatives [f]–[v] and the two stops [d]–[t], all that is necessary is to place the tip of the tongue between the teeth and breathe out gently ([θ] and [ð] are interdental consonants, whereas the others are dental, labio-dental and alveolar).
  - the consonant [h], wrongly referred to as 'aspirated H', is actually produced by releasing air from the mouth in the same manner as people do in winter when they wish to see their breath: *high, here, behind,* etc.

Stress and rhythm

Stress is a fundamental part of English, whereas its importance is often negligible in other languages. Stress is used to highlight certain syllables. As far as words are concerned in French, the last syllable is lightly stressed (*'un plastique', 'un éléphant', 'un ascenseur'*) without the other syllables and the vowels they contain being affected in any way whatsoever by this stress. The situation in English is completely different. The word *table* contains a vowel 'a', pronounced [eɪ] ([teɪbl]) when stressed, whereas there is practically no vowel sound in the word *comfortable* apart from in the first heavily stressed syllable ([ˈkʌmftəbl]).

This phenomenon affects monosyllabic words as well, including many of the grammatical words (prepositions, articles, conjunc-

tions, auxiliaries, pronouns), which are more often than not unstressed and pronounced in their 'weak form'. For example:

'You can come in' compared to 'You can'
   [ə]   [æ]
'Wait and see' compared to 'And now listen carefully'
   [ə]   [æ]

Generally speaking, the rhythm of a sentence in English is
profoundly influenced by the predominance of the stressed syllables, which leads to the unstressed syllables being delivered at a
faster rate (the impression that 'the English speak too quickly'). In
the four sentences which follow only two of the syllables are
stressed (the first and the last word) and the remainder of the
sentence consists of from one to four unstressed, atonic syllables:

Jill *is* **here.**   **Jill** *is a good* **girl.**
Jill *is a* **girl.**   **Jill** *isn't a good* **girl.**

The interesting thing about these four sentences is that they
each take approximately the same amount of time to say, no
matter how many atonic syllables occur between the stressed
ones.

Intonation

Intonation, which is often referred to as 'speech melody', has a
vital function in English, both in oral expression and in the
comprehension of spoken English. A famous American linguist has
shown that 'intonation patterns are more important in the comprehension of oral English than the phonetic quality of the sounds'
(Fries, 1945). Intonation is based on the relative pitch level of
syllables around the stressed syllables in a sentence. At these
points, the pitch can rise, or fall, or even combine these two
movements. Of particular importance is the role of the point
known as the nucleus (the tonic syllable), a syllable in an utterance
where a change of tone occurs, sometimes causing the following
syllables to stay at lower levels, even when the nucleus is located
at the beginning of the sentence:

All of them wanted to go.
\   • • – • • –

An experiment can be conducted which illustrates the point Fries
makes. When asking an unsuspecting English native speaker the
time, replace the question:

What time is it?
\   – • •

with the following sentence, using the same intonation but keeping
the French pronunciation:

Boîte à musique.

\\   —   •   •

Nine times out of ten, a reply like *It's five o'clock* or *It's half past ten*
will be the result!

The conclusion to be drawn from this is unavoidable: the quality
of intonation, and hence stress and rhythm, is a matter of the
utmost importance.

References and further reading

Fries, C. C., 1945. *Teaching and Learning English as a Foreign
Language*: University of Michigan Press.

Hawkins, E., 1984. *Awareness of Language: An Introduction*:
Cambridge University Press.

Jones, D., 1988. *English Pronouncing Dictionary* (14th edition,
revised by A. C. Gimson): Dent & Sons.

Leech, G. and J. Svartvik, 1975. *A Communicative Grammar of
English*: Longman.

Martinet, A., 1960. *Eléments de linguistique générale*: Armand
Colin.

Van Ek, J. and J. Trim, 1991. *Waystage*: Conseil de l'Europe,
Strasbourg, 1977: (2nd edition) Pergamon.

Appendix

Reference books

Dictionaries

For teachers

- MONOLINGUAL
  Longman Concise English Dictionary
  Oxford Advanced Learner's Dictionary
  Collins Cobuild English Language Dictionary

- BILINGUAL
  French–English
  Dictionnaire de poche: Robert–Collins
  Dictionnaire de l'anglais d'aujourd'hui: Presses Pocket
  Dictionnaire Compact: Harrap–Bordas

  German–English
  Großwörterbuch   Deutsch–Englisch/Englisch–Deutsch: Pons
  Collins
  Handwörtenbuch   Deutsch–Englisch/Englisch–Deutsch: Langens-
  cheidt

  Spanish–English
  English Learners Dictionary: Vox/Chambers
  Diccionario Collins Pocket: Collins
  Diccionario Collins Ingles: Collins

  Other languages (Italian–/Portuguese–English)
  Collins Compact or *Concise* dictionaries

For pupils

- MONOLINGUAL, ILLUSTRATED
  Basic Dictionary of English: Hachette
  Illustrated English Dictionary: Harrap
  Collins Picture Dictionary for Young Learners
  Puffin First Picture Dictionary

- BILINGUAL
  French–English
  Dictionnaire Gem: Hachette–Collins
  French Minidictionary: Oxford University Press
  Dictionnaire de l'anglais à l'école: Larousse

German–English
Großwörterbuch Deutsch–Englisch/Englisch–Deutsch: Pons Collins
Handwörterbuch Deutsch–Englisch/Englisch–Deutsch: Langenscheidt

Spanish–English
English Learners Dictionary: Vox/Chambers
Diccionario Collins Pocket: Collins
Diccionario Collins Ingles: Collins

Other Languages (Italian–/Portuguese–English)
Little Gem dictionaries: Collins
Italian Minidictionary: Oxford University Press

Grammars

For teachers
Quirk, R. and S. Greenbaum, 1973. *A University Grammar of English*: Longman.
Leech, G. and J. Svartvik, 1975. *A Communicative Grammar of English*: Longman.
Close, R. A., 1992. *A Teacher's Grammar*: Language Teaching Publications.

For French speakers
Girard, D., 1978. *Grammaire raisonnée de l'anglais*: Hachette.
Quenelle, G. and D. Hourquin, 1987. *6000 verbes anglais et leurs composés*: Hatier.

For Italian speakers
Capelle, G., Girard, D. D. Soulié and G. Soravia, 1982. *Basic English Grammar*: Principato.

For German speakers
Röhr, H., and B. Bartels, 1981. *The English Companion's Modern Grammar*: Diesterweg.
Ungerer, F., G. Meier, C. Schafer and S. Lechler, 1990. *A Grammar of Present-Day English*: Klett.

For Spanish speakers
Iglesias, M., 1991. *Gramatica Sucinta De La Lengua Inglesa*: Herder Gross.
Benedito, F., 1991. *Gramatica Inglesa*: Alhambra Longman.
Parkinson de Saz, S., 1989. *Gramatica Inglesa Basica*: Empeño 14.

Pronunciation dictionary

Jones, D., 1988. *English Pronouncing Dictionary*
(14th edition, revised by A. C. Gimson): Dent & Sons.

Teachers' books

There are still too few teacher's books written for teaching English
to young learners. This scarcity of books will not last long, however, as many new books are in the process of being written! You
will find the following publications particularly helpful:

Brewster, J. and A. Hughes, 1992. *Teaching English to Young
Learners: An Annotated Bibliography*: The British Council.
Brumfit, C., J. Moon and R. Tongue (eds.), 1991. *Teaching English
to Children: from Practice to Principle*: Collins.
CILT, 1990 onwards. *Pathfinder Series for Language Teachers*:
1–10. CILT.
Halliwell, S., 1992. *Teaching English in the Primary Classroom*:
Longman.
Kennedy, C. and J. Jarvis (eds.), 1991. *Ideas and Issues in Primary
ELT*: Nelson.
Scott, W. and L. Ytreberg, 1990. *Teaching English to Children*:
Longman.

The following series are generally useful to the language
teacher:

Handbooks for Language Teachers: Cambridge University Press
Practical Language Teaching: Heinemann
Keys to Language Teaching: Longman
Essential Language Teaching: Macmillan
Resource Books for Teachers: Oxford University Press

An invaluable source of ideas and techniques are the teacher's
books which accompany published materials for children. They
generally contain ideas for teaching vocabulary and grammar,
teaching the four language skills, using topics, songs, games,
roleplay, and so on.

The books listed below provide a wealth of ideas for teaching
English in the primary and secondary school. Not all have been
specifically written for ELT and young learners but you should be
able to adapt the ideas to your own teaching context.

Games, songs and rhymes

Astrop, J. and D. Byrne, 1981. *Games for Pairwork*: Cambridge University Press.

Beck, I. and K. King, 1985. *Oranges and Lemons*: singing and dancing games: Oxford University Press.

Byrne, D. and A. Waugh, 1982. *Jingle Bells and Other Songs* (+ cassette): Oxford University Press.

Carrier, M. et al., 1985. *Take 5: Games and Activities for the Language Learner*: Nelson.

Dakin, J., 1968. *Songs and Rhymes for the Teaching of English*: pupil's and teacher's books: Longman.

Graham, C., 1989. *Fairy Tale Jazz Chants*: Oxford University Press.

Lee, W. R., 1986. *Language Teaching Games and Contests* (3rd edition): Oxford University Press.

Matterson, E., 1969. *This Little Puffin . . .: Finger Plays and Nursery Games*: Puffin.

Retter, C. and N. Valls, 1984. *Bonanza: 77 English Language Games for Young Learners*: Longman.

Rixon, S., 1981. *How to Use Games in Language Teaching*: Macmillan.

Rixon, S., 1983. *Fun and Games*: Macmillan.

Ward, S., 1983. *Dippitydoo*: Activity book with cassette of songs: Longman.

Wright, A., D. Betteridge and M. Buckby, 1984. *Games for Language Learning*: Cambridge University Press.

Drawing and making things

Curtis, A. and J. Hindley, 1975. *The Knowhow Book of Paper Fun*: Usborne.

Kilroy, S., 1981. *Copycat*: drawing book: Puffin.

Kilroy, S., 1983. *Copycard*: make and draw your own cards: Puffin.

Kilroy, S., 1985. *Copyparty*: make your own party props: Puffin.

Kilroy, S., 1989. *Copythat*: a Copycat drawing book: Puffin.

Philpott, V. and M. Mcneil, 1975. *The Knowhow Book of Puppets*: Usborne.

Rosen, C., 1985. *Party Fun*: Usborne.

Tatchell, J., 1988. *How to Draw: Cartoons; Monsters; Animals and Machines*: Usborne.

Wright, A., 1984. *One Thousand Pictures for Teachers to Copy*: Collins/Addison Wesley.

Wright, A., 1989. *Pictures for Language Learners*: Cambridge University Press.

Using audio-visual aids

Allan, M., 1985. *Teaching English with Video*: Longman.

Byrne, D., 1980. *Using the Magnetboard*: Heinemann.

Mugglestone, P., 1980. *Planning and Using the Blackboard*: Heinemann.

Teaching vocabulary and grammar

Burridge, S. and J. Holderness, 1986. *Start with Words and Pictures* + pupil's activity book: Oxford University Press.

Gairns, R. and S. Redman, 1986. *Working with Words: A guide to teaching and learning vocabulary*: Cambridge University Press.

Harmer, J., 1987. *Teaching and Learning Grammar*: Longman.

Lee, W. R., 1984. *Opposites Set, Everyday Actions, Spatial Relationships, Things that Go Together, Tense Sequencing Cards, Prepositions, Body Parts, Clothes*: Language Development Aids.

Morgan, J. and M. Rinvolucri, 1988. *Vocabulary*: Oxford University Press.

Rinvolucri, M., 1984. *Grammar Games*: Cambridge University Press.

Ur, P., 1988. *Grammar Practice Activities*: Cambridge University Press.

Wallace, M. J., 1989. *Teaching Vocabulary*: Heinemann.

Watcyn-Jones, P., 1985. *Start Testing Your Vocabulary*: Penguin English.

Wright, A., 1984. *Picture Dictionary for Young Learners*: Collins.

Teaching listening and speaking

Brewster, J., 1991. 'Listening and the young learner' in *Teaching English to Children*, Brumfit, C., Moon, J. and Tongue, R. (eds.): Collins.

Bright Ideas Series, 1990. *Talking and Listening*: Scholastic Publications.

British Council, 1987. *English at the Primary Level*: Proceedings of the Sorrento Conference: Macmillan/Modern English Publications.

Byrne, D., 1987. *Techniques for Classroom Interaction*: Longman.

Dunn, O., 1983. *Beginning English with Children: Macmillan*.

Klippel, F., 1984. *Keep Talking*: communicative fluency activities for language teaching: Cambridge University Press.

Scott, W., 1980. *Are You Listening?*: pupil's and teacher's books: Oxford University Press.

Tench, P., 1981. *Pronunciation Skills*: Macmillan.

Ur, P., 1984. *Teaching Listening Comprehension*: Cambridge University Press.

Teaching reading and writing

Bright Ideas Series, 1985. *Spelling, Reading Activities, Developing Writing, Writing, Language Resources*: Scholastic Publications.

Brumfit, C., J. Moon and R. Tongue (eds.), 1991. *Teaching English to Children*: Collins.

Dunn, O., 1984. *Developing English with Young Learners*: Macmillan.

Hedge, T., 1985. *Using Readers in Language Teaching*: Macmillan.

Hedge, T., 1988. *Writing*: Oxford University Press.

Holden, S. (ed.), 1980. *Teaching Children*: Modern English Publications.

Mackay, D., B. Thompson and P. Schab, 1979. *Breakthrough to Literacy*: teacher's manual: Longman.

Nuttall, C., 1982. *Teaching Reading Skills in a Foreign Language*: Heinemann.

Wallace, C., 1988. *Learning to Read in a Multicultural Society: the social context of second language literacy*: Prentice-Hall.

Using the primary curriculum, topics and stories

Brewster, J., 1991. 'What is good primary practice?' in *Teaching English to Children*, Brumfit, C., Moon, J. and Tongue, R. (eds.): Collins.

Bright Ideas Series, 1988. *Project Teaching*: Scholastic Publications.

Ellis, G. and J. Brewster, 1991. *The Storytelling Handbook for Primary Teachers*: Penguin English.

Fried-Booth, D., 1986. *Project Work*: Oxford University Press.

Garvie, E., 1989. *Story as Vehicle*: Multilingual Matters.

Hester, H., 1983. *Stories in the Multilingual Classroom*: Harcourt Brace Jovanovich.

Morgan, J. and M. Rinvolucri, 1983. *Once Upon a Time: Using Stories in the Language Class*: Cambridge University Press.

Tann, C. S., 1988. *Developing Topic Work in the Primary School*: Falmer Press.

Journals, magazines and newspapers

Standpoints: a magazine for teachers of English containing articles of general interest, book reviews and a special section, Focus on the Classroom, which provides teachers with ideas for classroom activities. This includes a special section for young beginners. Published five times a year.

Subscriptions: CNDP/Abonnements
             BP 107–05

75224 Paris Cedex 05
France

Practical English Teaching: a magazine for teachers of English as a foreign language, containing book reviews and articles from teachers around the world on aspects of classroom practice. Published four times a year.

Subscriptions: MGP Ltd
Brookhampton Lane
Kineton
Warwick CV35 0JB
UK

Modern English Teacher: a magazine of practical ideas for teaching English as a foreign language from teachers around the world. Published four times a year.

Subscriptions: Subscriptions Manager (MET)
Macmillan
Houndmills
Basingstoke
Hants RG21 2XS
UK

JET: a new magazine for teachers of English as a foreign language to primary school children, containing news, a pull-out resource section based on a theme, and practical teaching ideas as well as more theoretical articles on current methodology, and materials reviews.

Subscriptions: MGP Ltd
Brookhampton Lane
Kineton
Warwick CV35 0JB
UK

BBC English: a magazine containing information on times and frequencies of BBC English broadcasts, home study sections, articles on grammar, usage and literature. Published four times a year.

Subscriptions: BBC English
PO Box 96
Cambridge
England

The Young Learners Newsletter: published by the IATEFL Young Learners Special Interest Group. Contains articles addressing practical and theoretical issues, news and book reviews.

Subscriptions: International Association for Teachers of English as
              a Foreign Language (IATEFL)
              3 Kingsdown Chambers
              Kingsdown Park
              Tankerton
              Whitstable
              Kent CT5 2DJ
              England

Language Matters: a magazine for primary teachers, containing practical ideas for the classroom and book reviews.

Subscriptions: Centre for Language in Primary Education
              Webber Row Teacher's Centre
              Webber Row
              London SE1 8QW
              England

English Language Teaching Journal: an international journal for teachers of English to speakers of other languages. It contains articles from around the world and aims to bridge the gap between the everyday concerns of teachers in their classrooms and the various disciplines such as psychology, sociology, and linguistics that may offer significant insights. Published four times a year.

Subscriptions: Journals Subscriptions Dept.
              Oxford University Press
              Pinkhill House
              Southfield Road
              Eynsham
              Oxford OX8 1JJ
              England

EFL Gazette: a newspaper for teachers of English as a foreign language with news from around the world, book reviews and teaching tips.

Subscriptions: EFL Gazette Subs.
              10 Wrights Lane
              London W8 6TA
              England

The Times Educational Supplement: published every Friday.

Subscriptions: TES
                Priory House
                St John's Lane
                London EC1M 4BX
                England

Further education for teachers: useful addresses

The British Council

There is a British Council in many countries and an English Studies Officer who is available to give advice about the teaching of English within the country, provide information about teacher-training courses and conferences, and any useful literature available.

The British Council in England provides a data bank of information on the teaching of English as a foreign language in general and on early learning.

The British Council
English Language Division
Medlock Street
Manchester
M15 4PR
England

IATEFL (International Association of Teachers of English as a Foreign Language)
IATEFL organizes a large annual conference as well as meetings and symposia for Special Interest Groups (SIGs). The teaching of English to young learners is one such group. It publishes a newsletter and has affiliated national associations in numerous European countries.

IATEFL
3 Kingsdown Chambers
Kingsdown Park
Tankerton
Whitstable
Kent
England CT5 2DJ

TESOL (Teachers of English to Speakers of Other Languages)
This organization is based in the United States at 1600 Cameron

Street, Suite 300, Alexandra, Virginia 22314–27705, USA. Its annual congress brings together thousands of participants from all over the world. There are national associations in a number of countries.

FIPLV (Fédération Internationale des Professeurs de Langues Vivantes)
This organization is based in Switzerland at Seestrasse 247, CH-8038 Zurich. It is a world confederation which gathers together most of the national associations of teachers of modern languages, as well as big international monolingual associations such as the two mentioned above.

The Council of Europe
This organization has been known for several decades for its important work in modern languages. Its present programme has the teaching of languages in primary schools as one of its priority areas. For further information, write to:

The Council of Europe
Modern Languages Section
BP431 R6
67006 Strasbourg
France

The European Community

Bureau LINGUA
10 rue du Commerce
B-1040 Brussels

CILT (Centres for Information on Language Teaching and Research)

Regent's College
Inner Circle
Regent's Park
London
NW1 4NS
ENGLAND